The Growing Minister

The Growing Minister

His Opportunities and Obstacles

Andrew W. Blackwood

Abingdon Press
NEW YORK • NASHVILLE

THE GROWING MINISTER

Library of Congress Catalog Card Number: 60-9194

PRINTED IN THE UNITED STATES OF AMERICA

In grateful recollection

of fifty years

with the author of *The Pastor's Wife*

Preface

THIS BOOK HAS GROWN OUT OF MY EXPERIENCES AT MINISTERIAL conferences and my correspondence with many pastors. In the last decade or so I have met with groups of clergymen in half the states of the Union, and in parts of Canada. I have corresponded with pastors in all these and most other parts of the two countries. Everywhere I have found ministers sincere, earnest, and high-minded. I have also found them concerned and perplexed, not so much about preaching and related concerns, but about their own spiritual lives, and their spiritual contribution to the work of the Kingdom. By spirituality I mean Christlikeness.

More than at any time in my experience I sense among ministers a yearning to be like their Lord. Among older denominations, as among "newer churches," I feel that pastors are ready and eager for a new advance in spirituality, and that for the loftiest ends. In attempting to meet this need I have relied largely on the Scriptures, and on recorded experiences of ministers throughout church history. Unfortunately, I have found in print comparatively little about the sort of minister who most needs encouragement. I refer to the pastor of a church not large, and nowise conspicuous.

The entire undertaking has proved to be unexpectedly difficult. Among all the books I have written for ministers this one has cost me most. Apart from such old standbys as Richard Baxter's *Reformed Pastor* (1656) and William Law's *Serious Call to a Devout and Holy Life* (1729), I have found in print relatively little about the way the Lord uses a pastor's routine work to make him a better man. Self-improvement should never become his chief aim in life. But if a pastor lives and works for the glory of God and the service of men, personal improvement will come as a by-product.

My chief difficulty has been with myself. In the first half of the book I point to ideals that I have not reached. In the latter half I deal with various obstacles, some of which I still must face. For many such reasons my heart goes out to pastors with whom I may seem to find fault. Frankly, I have followed an old Scottish adage: "Remember your own sins and charge them on the congregation. Then you will hit every man in the house!"

In their loftiest form the ideals of a growing minister shine out in the New Testament, not least in the Book of Acts and in early parts of II Corinthians. As for obstacles that every pastor must face, many of them appear in the Pastoral Epistles. For encouragement and help in seeing how these truths bear on the growth of a pastor, I feel grateful to former students and countless other pastors who have taught me much; to editors and librarians who have given me expert counsel; and to my wife and sons who have helped me in ways distinctly their own.

Most of all do I render thanks to the Heavenly Father who has given me work to do and strength to do it, as I "nightly pitch [my] moving tent a day's march nearer home." (Phil. 3:13-15 R.S.V.)

ANDREW W. BLACKWOOD

Contents

PART ONE
Opportunities to Grow

PART TWO
Obstacles to Growth

PART ONE

Opportunities to Grow

CHAPTER I

Ministerial Ideals

UNDER GOD, THE USEFULNESS AND THE GROWTH OF A MINISTER depend on his ideals. Here we shall take for granted that a certain pastor has had a personal experience of redeeming grace, that he has received a call to the ministry, and that he wishes to render the largest possible service. Other writers have dealt with such a ministry broadly, often in the plural. Here we shall think mainly about one person, typical of many. This friend may be a pastor here at home, a missionary overseas, or a young man making ready for such a life work.

What personal ideals ought such a man to cherish? In its form the answer may come from a master preacher, James S. Stewart, of Edinburgh. His volume of sermons, *The Gates of New Life,* includes a striking message, "Why Be a Christian?" The answer appears in four words which stand out below. Since they now serve a different purpose, the four adjectives appear in a different order, with the most important one first. Since my four attendant statements seem to be almost self-evident, they call for little comment.

The Highest Work in the World

The calling of a Christian minister is *higher* than that of any other man on earth. All honor to anyone who serves God and men as a teacher, a physician, or in any other Christlike work. In "the days of His flesh" our Lord devoted Himself largely to service as Teacher and Healer of body and mind. But to us now He stands out far more as the Ideal Minister. To serve as a pastor means to grow more and more like Him. What other calling on earth could be so high? For instance, listen to William

Carey, pioneer missionary to India. Once in later years he wrote that his son Felix had turned away from an opportunity to be a missionary and had shriveled up to become an ambassador of Great Britain.

A pastor represents men before God. In private and in public whenever he prays for others he voices their needs, desires, and aspirations. For such a privilege how can he ever feel worthy? "Prayer time," said Frederick W. Faber, "is God's punishment time." Especially during the celebration of the Lord's Supper a pastor may have an overwhelming sense of personal insufficiency. "It is then," writes Arthur J. Gossip, "that our disloyalties come home to roost. I don't know that our sins ever look so ghastly as they do at Christ's Table, when we seem to soil the very vessels with our touch, and are afraid that we may block the rush of God's grace to His people." [1]

At a local Methodist church a massive golden cross surmounts the altar. There as a visiting minister I have often stood to consecrate the offerings of the waiting throng. When they all arose to sing the long meter doxology I could see my face reflected in that cross. Then as never before I understood why the noblest of our hymns leads one to declare: "When I survey the wondrous Cross, . . . I pour contempt on all my pride."

In many ways a clergyman also represents God before men. As a preacher and as a man, not only does he stand out in the community as a living representative of the local church, but he likewise represents the "holy Church throughout the world," and the far more vast Kingdom of God. By his life and walk among men, his conduct of a community funeral, and his dinner talk at a Rotary Club, he can help to make God and His Kingdom seem momentous or momentary. Hence it seems that the highest privilege of a minister today is to represent God before men.

[1] See *In Christ's Stead,* Warrack Lectures (New York: George H. Doran Co., 1925), p. 41.

The Hardest Work on Earth

The calling of a minister is likewise *harder* than that of any other mortal. This has always been the case, and perhaps never so much as now. Among various factors that make a clergyman's work difficult today let us think of only two. First, he lives in a new "atomic age" when the thoughts and fears of men keep swiftly changing. Within the past decade or so thinking men everywhere have begun to use a new vocabulary, with novel words about demonic forces that may soon be released to scourge the earth, if not to destroy our so-called civilization.

Again, the pastor lives and works in a time when the so-called civilized world has become increasingly secular. In our own country crime has increased—notably among teen-agers. Millions of homes seem to be disintegrating. Partly because of television, radio, and other noteworthy inventions, the thoughts of children and adults have turned toward guns and "gunplay," liquor and gambling, with less and less about the ideals of "mother, home, and heaven."

For a while after World War II we all welcomed a "return to religion." During a single year almost ten million persons in our land bought new copies of the Bible. Church attendance increased, and contributions reached a new height. Books somewhat religious became best sellers. Newspapers and magazines formerly full of filth began to bow their heads at the name of the Church. Of late this "rising tide of religion" seems to have been receding. About all of these appraisals thoughtful men may differ. However, everyone who knows the facts today will agree that it is harder now than ever for a pastor to get people to pray and to engage in personal work.

The parish ministry today is difficult basically for the same reason as before our "atomic age," with its "sensate civilization." Unlike other professional men, a minister has to deal mainly with souls. To deal with a soul means to show deep concern about the spiritual welfare of a person made in the image of God, with potential power to become like Him, or else like the devil. Whenever a clergyman prays, preaches, makes a sick call, or counsels with a friend in distress, God's local representative is serving the highest interests of a soul, bound for heaven or for hell.

The difficulty and the delicacy seem to increase when we think about his dealing directly with sin. Sin means any wrong relation, or lack of right relation, between a man and God. Such lack of "rightness" also involves wrong relations with others, and within a man himself (Rom. 7:13-25). Here again, the black facts defy description, largely because they have to do with unconscious depths. Even so, a pastor's main work has to do with human beings, every one of whom stands in some relation to his own sins, and to those of others.

Once again, a minister has much to do with sickness, whether of the mind, the body, or both. So has a physician or a surgeon, but not in any such deep and abiding sense as a physician of souls, or it may be, a surgeon of the soul. Who but a man of God can diagnose a case where sin affects both mind and body, and where the cure can come only through the healing touch of Christ's dear hand? On the other side, who has so many opportunities to bungle and be guilty of the deadliest malpractice in the healing of souls? In the words of Macbeth,

> Canst thou not minister to a mind diseas'd,
> Pluck from the memory a rooted sorrow,
> Raze out the written troubles of the brain,
> And with some sweet oblivious antidote
> Cleanse the stuff'd bosom of that perilous stuff
> Which weighs upon the heart? (V, 3, 37-42)

A minister's work is most difficult because he has to deal with sorrow. The stroke of death may have come to bereave a home yesterday, or the shadow may have been deepening for twenty years. As Joseph Parker used to say at the City Temple in London, "Every pew has at least one broken heart." According to a brilliant Wesleyan divine, W. L. Watkinson, beneath the outer garments of many a man there is a hidden sackcloth, a silent symbol of grief that never will let go. Whatever the facts in the case, it is the minister's calling to lead the sorrowing friend out into the sunlight where he will have a heart full of love and joy, peace and hope, all through belief in the crucified, risen, and ever-present Lord.

In presenting to young men the claims of the Gospel ministry we ought always to stress the difficulties, as well as the delights. Difficult tasks appeal to the strength, the courage, and the idealism of a young man who has begun to follow Christ, the Christ who once "set His face like a flint," going up to Jerusalem, there to die. As a rule it seems better for us older folk to let Christ do the calling into His ministry. On the day I was born I was dedicated to this life work, but I never discovered the fact until after I had been ordained. Later as a teacher I found it difficult to help prepare for the ministry a young man called only by his mother. Probably she did not stress the difficulty.

One day while fairly young I was driving to see persons in distress of various sorts. With me in the car was a lad of seven years. When he saw a billboard lauding the athletic stunts of Douglas Fairbanks, the boy asked: "Can you climb a steep wall like that?" "No, I could not even find the toeholds. But I can do things that Fairbanks would not dare to do." Seeing that the boy looked incredulous, I went on: "In that last home a young wife had a little baby who was born dead. Now she knows from the doctors that she and her husband can never have another child. What could Douglas Fairbanks do to help those broken hearts?" Later that son became a minister, but not because either parent had ever made any such suggestion, or presented the ministry as an easy life. Ease appeals only to weaklings.

The Holiest Mission Among Men

The calling of a minister ought to be *holier* than that of any other mortal. In the Bible sense, holiness means being like God in sinless perfection, and unlike men in love of sinning. Holiness has far more to do with God's goodness, love, and mercy than with His power, wisdom, and glory. Holiness calls for being like Jesus our Lord, who dwelt among men and was ever one of them, in all save weaknesses and sins. While our God wishes all His redeemed children to be holy, He would have a minister set the others a living example that they can follow Godward.

The word spiritual says much the same. This in turn means being filled with the Holy Spirit. It should seem natural to think of any pastor as a spiritual person. On the contrary when a young kinsman of mine recently went to do graduate work in a world-famous divinity school abroad, an intelligent young lady seriously asked the young man's wife if her husband had ever been converted, or if he had taken up the ministry as what we would call a "racket." Once a friend asked William James what he meant by a spiritual man. That expert in the use of words replied that he could not define the term, but that he could show what it meant. Then he pointed to Phillips Brooks.

A pastor needs to be holy for many reasons. Among them take this: he has constantly to deal with sinful men, without ever seeming to be like them in experience of present sinfulness. After he has lived in a community long enough to be known as spiritual, he ought to share the secrets of one breaking heart after another, each of them eager to confide in a friend who will not seem shocked, but will lead out into the sunlight where God makes His home. In all this ministry of "salvaging souls," a man needs to have a present experience of the Cross with its transforming power.

A pastor ought also to live among worldly men, as a friend and helper, without ever seeming worldly. In the Scriptures this word, often abused, means living for self, for things, for pleasure—all as ends in themselves; not living for God, for others, and for usefulness. (See I John 2:15-17; Matt. 13:22-23.) Worldliness may show itself in countless petty ways, but worldliness itself has little to do with such matters as the moderate enjoyment of motion pictures, or watching television on Sunday. Theoretically, worldliness means that a man's working philosophy includes no God but himself, or the things that God has made. Practically, worldliness usually means undue love of money, or of pleasure.

It is harder to win for Christ and goodness a man or a woman who is worldly than one who is out-and-out wicked. So declared Frederick W. Robertson, minister of an Anglican church at Brighton, a fashionable watering place on the English Channel. There he witnessed the daily parade of worldlings who were experimenting with all of earth's substitutes for God and His Good News. When Robertson dealt with a self-confessed sinner, the clergyman nearly always found a sense of need, and a desire for better things. But with many a worldling, drugged by indulgence in pagan delights, there was no sense of loss and and no desire for improvement. Whatever the facts about the other person, how can a minister help unless he himself has a present experience of Christ's transforming power?

A pastor likewise has to do with the weak. And yet he himself must never seem weak in faith. Like his Master, who was the Divine Servant (Isa. 42:3-4), a minister often has to bind up a broken reed, and fan smoking flax into a beautiful flame. In the Hebrew form these words say that in ministering to the weak and the disconsolate, the Lord's servant must never give way to weakness, or to discouragement. All the while he should look on the world through the other man's eyes, feel as he ought to feel, and do the will of God in leading this friend into the peace and strength of the Most High.

Once again, and still more strangely, a pastor needs to be holy because he often has to do with saints of God, and yet both he and they know that he has not yet begun to feel saintly. If his activity with the young, the well, and the strong leaves him time to visit bed-ridden saints, how can he seem at home in a quiet upper room? At least he can learn how to listen. Little by little he may begin to enjoy what W. E. Sangster of London calls "the language of Canaan," which may refer to "Beulah Land" and Bunyan's "Celestial Mountains." In humble upper rooms more than one young pastor has taken a postgraduate course in the biblical meaning of holiness unto the Lord.

At first a young dominie may feel hurt when he learns that some of the saints keep praying for the deepening of his spiritual life. Dwight L. Moody felt so about two women in Chicago who were praying that he would enter more fully into "the secret of the Lord." Knowing that they were neither self-righteous nor censorious, and that they loved him, the young evangelist, who was already beginning to be a power for God, began to keep his heart open to every breeze from heaven. At the age of thirty-five he entered into a fuller experience of transforming grace. So did John Wesley, and so did Thomas Chalmers, who stands in the forefront of all Presbyterian pastor-preachers. In time each of those three became a Protestant saint.

The Happiest Life Here Below

Last of all, the life of a pastor ought to be *happier* than that of any other man. According to a Scottish professor of theology, who had watched a host of active ministers, a pastor's enjoyment of his God-given duties goes far to make his life work effective. Perhaps unfortunately, the reverse holds true. In the history of the Church thus far, with few exceptions, the most effective all-round "pastoral directors" have enjoyed the work that some brethren have simply endured as a matter of duty. Like Sir Wilfred Grenfell, missionary to Labrador, many a pastor far more obscure can exclaim to people who try to console him: "Don't pity me! I'm having the time of my life!" On the other hand, more than a few hard-working parsons could double their effectiveness if they learned how to feel happy and look radiant. (See Phil. 4:4.)

As a witness hear Richard Baxter who was far from strong and, like Paul, did well the practical work of several men: "What an excellent life it is to live in studying and preaching

Christ; to be still searching into His mysteries, and feeding on them; to be daily in the contemplation of the blessed nature, or works, or ways of God! . . . Our employments are all high and spiritual. Whether we be alone or with others, our business is for another world. Oh, but were our hearts more suitable to this work, what a blessed, joyful life we should lead!" [2]

In coming chapters we shall look at various sectors in the routine of a "pastoral director." Just now let us resolve to view them all as opportunities and privileges, not as burdens to be accepted dutifully, and as tasks to be done grudgingly. With a pastor's giving of himself in work, as with a layman's giving of "his" money, the value depends largely on the spirit in which a man renders the service. In the use of time, energy, or any other God-given resource, blessing comes most of all to the "hilarious" giver. (See II Cor. 9:7*c,* Greek.)

All these pastoral joys spring largely from the fact that a minister serves as local custodian of the Gospel. Whatever he does, and however he does it, he ought to do it all because he desires to behold the triumph of the Gospel as the super-atomic energy of Almighty God. The utmost available power of atomic energy can only change the form and the position of things. But a minister of the Gospel has ever in hand a force waiting to change a drunkard into a sober man, an impure woman into one with a soul as white as the snow on Mount Hermon, a home mission community from a cesspool of iniquity into a worthy place to rear boys and girls, and an island in the South Pacific from an abode of cannibals into one of the most heavenly regions in the world.

Looking backward, let us think of a pastor's life as higher and harder, holier and happier than that of anyone else on earth. Some reader may protest: "All of that interests me as an ideal, and as a matter of history. But if Richard Baxter or Wilfred Grenfell were up against what I have to face at Tenth and

[2] See *The Reformed Pastor* (New York: Robert Carter, 1860), pp. 292-93. Original (1656) based largely on Acts 20:17-38.

Broadway (or out in Suburbia) he would not be so holy and he might not seem so happy! Why not be realistic?"

Amen! That is exactly what we ought to do. In the light of all these ideals, as they will later appear in detail, we shall look at the difficulties in the way of such a ministry now. Meanwhile, if any reader will study the life and times of Baxter or Grenfell, the student will conclude that few of us pastors here in the States know the meaning of difficulties and obstacles, not to speak of perils. In fact, when has any man of God ever become saintly while cultivating a field devoid of stones? So let us conclude that the Lord wishes each of us to be holy and happy in the field to which He has opened the gateway.

Let us remember too that He has a different sort of obstacles and difficulties for each of His ministering servants. Richard Baxter knew nothing about the hardships and perils that Grenfell would later find in Labrador. The latter may never have read about the burdens and trials that had attended Baxter in the heart of the tempestuous seventeenth century. Neither of them, I judge, could have excelled in the field where the other one labored. So if any pastor feels that he ought to receive sympathy because of what he now suffers in a field full of stones, he will surely find sympathy in the Christ of the Cross, who still keeps saying, as He once told Peter and other future apostles:

If any man will come after me, let him deny himself, and take up his cross daily, and follow me. (Luke 9:23.)

CHAPTER II

Personality Power

THE IDEALS OF A GROWING MINISTER RELATE, MOST OF ALL, TO the glory of God. They likewise relate to the caliber of a man's personality. Personality here means all of a minister as he appears to others. This way of using the term comes from Paul E. Johnson, a foremost writer about the psychology of religion. With others at the Boston University School of Theology he upholds the Philosophy of Personalism, which makes everything center around personality and persons, both human and divine. As for his use of "person," we shall think about that later. Under God, a pastor's usefulness depends on his personality.

Personality should have nothing to do with showmanship of gifts and powers that come from God. Personality of a Christian sort cannot be acquired in a "charm school," with a ten-week course in "how to win friends and influence people." That sort of thing may have a limited place on the stage, but not in the ministry. Let us rather think of personality as the "outside view" of a man like a prophet or an apostle. Ideally, it appeared in Christ as He moved among men.

So let us think about a thesis, or proposition: on the human level a pastor's usefulness depends on his personality. If so, the increase of his effectiveness depends on the growth of his personality. This truth stands out in a poem called "Renascence," by Edna St. Vincent Millay:

> The world stands out on either side
> No wider than the soul is wide;
> Above the earth is stretched the sky,—
> No higher than the soul is high.

The heart can push the sea and land
Farther away on either hand;
The soul can split the sky in two,
And let the face of God shine through.
But East and West can pinch the heart
That can not keep them pushed apart;
And he whose soul is flat—the sky
Will cave in on him by and by.[1]

The influence of personality appears in every aspect of a pastor's work today. For example, take preaching. In the well-known words of Phillips Brooks, "Preaching is the bringing of truth through personality." "Truth" here means a message from God voiced by a chosen messenger to meet some vital need of the hearers, especially the need arising from sin.

Power in the Pulpit

History and present-day experience show that in the pulpit a man's effectiveness depends on his personality. In our time the stress falls on Brooks's term about preaching as "communication." Some of us prefer to think of a minister as dwelling in Bunyan's "house of the interpreter." Not only does the ambassador of God "communicate" the message; as an "interpreter" he ought also to make clear what it means in terms of human need today. Whatever the description of pulpit work, it all has to do with the speaker's personality. God meant it to be so.

The phrase, "truth through personality," suggests that preaching calls for a high degree of intelligence. It also requires the use of emotion, under the control of a Christ-centered will. Pulpit work ought always to consist of worthy thoughts surcharged with feeling. Not only must the spokesman for God understand what he is to say during the coming hour, he must also know how to make it all clear, luminous, and effective in

[1] Copyright 1912-1940 by Edna St. Vincent Millay. From *Collected Poems*, Harper & Brothers. By permission of Norma Millay Ellis.

the heart and life of the hearer. Week after week, it may be with more than one sermon every Lord's Day, such mental activity calls for the diligent use of all a man's intellectual powers, after they have been highly trained.

The Church often underestimates the intellectual requirements of a parish minister, not least in the pulpit. Personally, I cherish a high regard for scholars, of whom I have known few, as distinct from mere masters of book learning. Having devoted my earlier years of manhood to the pastorate, and my later years to seminary teaching, I have found that it requires more intellectual ability and creativeness to be a useful pastor-preacher than to be an acceptable seminary professor. For instance, take biblical theology, a subject that I once taught long enough to know its difficulty and its fascination. In the Bible and in learned books now on my shelves I can soon find all the materials necessary to prepare for a classroom discussion of any Christian doctrine as it appears in the writings of Peter or Paul.

This last year and more I have served as acting minister of a suburban church. Again and again, as in former times, I have come across pastoral and preaching problems where no learned books have shown me how to proceed. For example, having lived in the South long enough to love the people and the churches there, how can I preach about the removal of race prejudice (Acts 10) here in a city where such intelligent preaching is much needed just now? In another city years ago, every clerk on the main business street was tempted to cheat from his employer so as to gamble at the local race track. How could I prepare a biblical sermon about the sin and the folly of gambling?

In many such cases I had to choose one of two courses. Either I could use my brains or else I could dodge the issue. Only an arrant coward would refuse to obey God's call for a message in keeping with a crying need of the hour. For various reasons I have found it almost as difficult to prepare an evangelistic sermon as an ethical or a doctrinal one. In fact, if a preacher wishes to keep using biblical truth to meet the heart needs of men and women today, with their boys and girls, he must have brains to use, and then employ them all in the service of the God from whom they have come. In as far as I can judge from experience and wide observation, all of this difficulty has increased since World War II.

Whenever a worthy pastor goes into the pulpit he wishes to deliver a good sermon. A good sermon here means one that does the hearers good in their present situation. Such a minister ought to keep growing in pulpit effectiveness. The lives of pulpit masters in earlier days, and the experience of others now at work, all make clear that the way to improve in preaching ability is to keep using all of one's intellectual powers and resources. At thirty-five a man ought to preach better than when he was ordained. And so on through each passing decade. This is no small part of what one means by being a growing minister.

Power in Public Worship

Leading in the public worship of God likewise tests the power of a man's personality. But the various acts of leading in corporate worship—other than the Scripture lesson and the sermon—call for the controlled expression of feeling, rather than thought. In any statement of the sort one tends to make the facts seem far too simple. In public prayer as in preaching a man has to employ all his God-given abilities. Still it holds true that when preparing to pray in church, as when selecting the hymns, or making ready to lead in a responsive reading, a minister has to employ his emotions much more than his intelligence. Perhaps I should also refer to his imagination, which has to do largely with feeling, though never apart from "the kindly light of reason," and the control of a Christian will.

As a witness turn to Jonathan Edwards, a man with perhaps the mightiest brain power thus far in the American church. In his *Treatise Concerning the Religious Affections* (1746)—the most interesting of his major works now being edited and reprinted at Yale—this philosopher and theologian shows that in Christianity the heart has more to do than the head. With this point of view Paul would have agreed, and so would the apostle John. And yet some current books about the pastor deal mainly with his intellect. Really we ought to think of him as a strong all-round personality, like his Lord.

Especially does leading in public prayer call for the controlled expression of Christian feeling.[2] Among all the prayers in the Bible, or in the *Book of Common Prayer,* no one has ever discovered a "form of sound words" devoid of emotion. Among those of us who believe in "free worship," which means liberty to employ or not to employ historic forms of prayer, this part of public worship is "the offering up of our desires unto God." So declares the Westminster *Shorter Catechism.* Whether a given prayer voices adoration or confession, thanksgivings or petitions for those present, intercessions for persons elsewhere or dedication to Christian service—in every case emotion should prevail. This may be why a "teaching prayer" or a "preaching prayer" often seems as cold and remote as "Greenland's icy mountains."

Like every other gift that comes down from above, ability to lead in worship should grow through the years. If so, the improvement will come largely through the broadening, deepening, and enriching of the leader's personality, especially in the cultivation of his finer emotions. Above all, such growth in the service of God appears when a minister leads in Baptism, or at the Lord's Supper. Only as a man becomes more like the Lord Jesus can he hope to excel in these most delicate and exacting of his earthly ministries, when a mortal redeemed by grace leads others far into the King's country, and there causes them to feel "lost in wonder, love, and praise."

[2] See my *Leading in Public Prayer* (Nashville: Abingdon Press, 1958).

Power as a Pastor

All the ministries so far ought to be pastoral. Still we can employ the term with special reference to what a man does for God outside pulpit and study. For example, take pastoral counseling. As a rule a young minister, or a man new on the field, must wait a while before he can have many opportunities for personal counseling. For much the same reason a missionary new in Japan has to learn the language and the local customs before he can work effectively with the Japanese. Whether at home or overseas, the value of what a minister does in a man-to-man conference depends on the breadth and caliber of his personality. If through the years he continues to grow through exercise of all his Godgiven powers, he will also keep improving as a pastoral counselor.

After a brief course in counseling a senior in the seminary may get the idea that he can quickly diagnose almost every case of soul distress. By use of modern "techniques" he expects regularly to bring about release and heart's ease. A trained psychiatrist works more deliberately, but some mentors of young ministers seem to cure all their book cases at a single interview. Such has not been the experience of us older men, as it was not the case with men who stand out in the Bible as personal counselors. Pastors in every age have engaged in counseling, often under other names. Today any minister does wisely to secure the best available training. Even then he will have to rely largely on his own spiritual resources, especially his feeling of empathy.

Take the matter of drunkenness, for example. On the fingers of one hand I can count the number of alcoholics whom I have helped to lead into permanent sobriety. The same has held true with cases of impending divorce, and need of reconciliation. In most cases the failure may have been due to not knowing how to put myself into the other person's place emotionally, looking at his world from his point of view, and then encouraging him to do what he should in finding his way out into the sunlight.

Much of this I have learned by watching the methods of untutored workers in Alcoholics Anonymous. In short, a pastoral counselor must have a heart.

All the while the Lord expects a pastor to serve as friend and counselor to many persons too timid or fearful to come for a personal interview. In the average community today there are more lonely persons and troubled homes than at any time in our American history. Such persons and families need a pastor, in the older sense of the term. In the opinion of many thoughtful laymen, this is where the "average" minister of today fails most often. Methods may change, as they should, and difficulties seem to increase. But if a man has the heart of a shepherd he loves people. He knows his own people, personally and well. If they do not come to him, he goes to them.

What a minister does for people, one by one, or in a family group, depends on his personality. For this reason, as a man becomes more Christlike, he grows in ability to help people in their homes. For example, how can he advise them about a mongoloid son who has become too strong physically to be kept at home with smaller children? Sometimes, like Paul, a minister can help most by having tears unshed. But they must not be crocodile tears. Once in a while a pastor complains because people do not notify him about serious illness or a household calamity. If so, he should ask himself to what degree he excels in "the art of ministering to the sick," or in bringing the peace of God to a distraught family.

Like many another saint of God, Richard Baxter became increasingly Christlike through being an indefatigable pastor. Somehow that did not interfere with his work in the pulpit, or with his writing an incredible number of books. In *The Reformed Pastor* he pleaded for the faithful shepherding of adults, as well as boys and girls. In response to the objection that there was not time enough for pastoral calling, he spoke out bluntly, in words that voice what many of our most spiritual laymen feel today:

If you have so much greater business that you cannot ordinarily have time to do the minister's work, you should not undertake the office, for ministers are "men separated to the Gospel of Christ," and must give themselves wholly to these things.

Usually we think of a pastor as dealing with people one at a time, or else in a family group. In Bible days a shepherd also excelled in leading the flock as a whole. Without going further into the matter here, let us note that a minister's ability as a practical leader depends on his personality. Such increasing effectiveness, under God, comes through development of his personality. Not in books or through teachers can he learn how to size up a given situation; envision what the Lord wishes people to do amid these conditions; lead them to desire what the Lord wishes them to accomplish; enlist lay leaders whom the people will gladly follow; encourage all concerned to persevere until they complete the work in God's way; and then ascribe the credit wherever credit is due.

In the right sort of pastoral ministry ability to lead develops through the years. This is because the pastor becomes more and more like the "Master Workman of our race." Indeed, as we shall see in due time, pastoral leadership may become as truly a means of grace as any other way in which a man grows like his Lord. How otherwise did John Wesley continue to grow in grace throughout the fifty years when he was laying the foundations of the future Methodist Church?

Power Beyond the Community

As the years go by a pastor should have opportunities for Christian usefulness beyond the home community. As a rule these openings come unsought. In any case the extent and the value of his influence depend on the richness and the appeal of his personality. Simply by gaining the good will, the confidence, and the admiration of men, a village pastor may influence every person and home within a radius of ten miles, or even more.

The same holds true of a clergyman in a suburban field, or in the heart of a vast city. All the while, an equally able minister of a neighboring congregation may wield no such far-reaching influence. The difference seems to lie in the realm of personality.

Among all the "pastoral directors" whom I have known somewhat intimately, the one who impressed me most was George W. Truett, at the First Baptist Church of Dallas, Texas. Without in any way neglecting his own large congregation, he exerted a wholesome influence over that city, over that state, over the nation as a whole, notably in the South, and over certain areas across the Atlantic. From decade to decade his influence increased. Why so? Not because he sought anything of the sort, but because he had the kind of personality that called out from others their love and loyalty.

In a way far different Billy Graham has influenced countless persons who have never spoken to him directly. I have often heard him speak, read his books, and sought to ascertain the secret of his power. The answer seems to lie in two directions. One reply would refer everything good to his Lord, and in this answer Graham himself would heartily agree. The other would look for the secret in terms of personality. James M. Barrie calls it charm. In one of his most delightful plays someone asks the meaning of charm, and the leading character replies, in a form that I have altered by changing a single word, which is in italics:

"What *is* charm?" . . . "Oh . . . it's a sort of bloom on a *minister*. If you have it, you don't need to have anything else; and if you don't have it, it doesn't matter much what else you have." [3]

The whimsical Scotsman states the facts too simply. Even so, Barrie himself had charm of personality. So has Billy Graham. And so, in a fashion all his own, has every pastor who rightly influences people. In view of these facts about the importance

[3] See *Representative Plays,* "What Every Woman Knows," ed. by Wm. Lyon Phelps (New York: Charles Scribner's Sons, 1918), p. 198.

of a minister's personality let us think about its development. Strange as the fact may seem, no pastor can make himself over into a more attractive and effective personality. Many of us used to try, but we failed, most dismally. In a real sense a pastor retires with essentially the same kind of personality that he had when he was ordained.

By the grace of God, however, any real minister can make the most of himself as a person. Thus he should keep on growing more Christlike as long as he lives. Note the distinction between "personality," which a minister cannot change by his utmost efforts, and "person"—one who is able to improve himself year after year. This way of thinking comes from Paul E. Johnson,[4] though he is not responsible for the use I am to make of the distinction between "personality" and "person." "Personality" means what a minister is when viewed from without, and "person" means what he is when viewed from within. "Man looketh on the outward appearance [the personality], but the Lord looketh on the heart [the person]." (I Sam. 16:7*b*.)

Every reader wishes to keep growing as a Christlike person. What steps should a young minister take in order to become more and more like his Lord? Let him daily put himself in the hands of God and then keep using such means of grace as will appear in the succeeding chapters. Year by year he will continue to grow. All the while God will take care of his personality. Hence he will become more and more effective in ministry among men. But such growth in personality will come only as a by-product of increasing Christlikeness.

On paper all of this may seem paradoxical. In everyday experience the theory works. It never fails. Try it, in faith! If you keep taking first-class care of yourself as a Christlike person, God will take first-class care of your Christian personality. Remember that "personality" means the way in which you in-

[4] See *Personality and Religion* (Nashville: Abingdon Press, 1957), pp. 26-27.

fluence others, as a rule without conscious effort on your part. But "person" means what you are in the eyes of God. As a person you can keep improving, by careful planning and by daily routine. For the sake of Christ and His Church determine to make the most of yourself as a person like your Lord.

CHAPTER III

Devotional Reading

LET US NOW THINK DIRECTLY ABOUT THE GROWTH OF A MINISTER spiritually. In Bible days an elderly apostle wrote to a friend, who may have been a young pastor about to enter his first charge: "Beloved, I wish above all things that thou mayest prosper and be in health, even as thy soul prospereth" (III John, vs. 2). These words suggest a devotional study about "The Health of a Pastor's Soul." Carrying out the idea in the text, we may think of a young minister as spiritually well and strong, not as needing any drastic surgery of the soul. If he wishes to keep growing in likeness to his Lord, he ought to have a daily regimen of soul food, fresh air, and spiritual exercise. Here we shall consider only the food for his soul.

Such food comes chiefly through devotional reading of the Bible. In his "morning watch" a pastor may at times delve into other books, notably the Hymnal. Here we can think only about the Scriptures, not in the way of intellectual study, which may occupy two or three hours later in the forenoon. Ideally, devotions call for an hour a day, six days in the week, preferably early in the morning. The reading ought to begin, continue, and end in the spirit of prayer, often in the act. The feeling throughout ought to be that of enjoying a privilege, not performing a duty. Imagine the sorry state of a minister who feels indifferent while communing with God through His written Word! What a way not to put God first!

The frank motive ought to be self-improvement, for the glory of God and the benefit of His people. "For Christ's sake, and for their sakes, I should make the most of myself through loving fellowship with Him in the Book." This is an echo of what our

Lord says about Himself in the heart of the "high-priestly prayer" (John 17:17, 19). Here the Lord Jesus dedicates Himself to His God-given mission, and pleads that future ministers may do the same. He prays that "through the truth" of God they may be prepared for life service much like His own. Today such transforming truth comes to a pastor through day-by-day reading of the Bible devotionally. To read devotionally ought to mean the use of a burning heart (Luke 24:32) and a seeing eye.

The spirtual value of such reading depends in part on keeping an hour free from the sort of intellectual labor that should attend the remainder of the morning. Hence a pastor with a hungry soul may for his devotional hour adopt a motto, which need not appear in a visible form: "No Hunting Allowed!" No searching after juicy texts ready for use. No looking for sermon materials to be laid away in a freezer. Some of that searching may come later in his study. Meanwhile let the servant of God enjoy an hour of fellowship with Him and His Book. Such was the daily custom of Alexander Maclaren, John Henry Jowett, and many another growing pastor in days not remote. Because of those morning hours of quiet devotion, such a minister came to know his Bible well, and to love it much. In a sense, he became "a man of one book."

Using the Book Method

The value of such reading depends also on the method. Experience shows that it is more profitable to follow a single method for ten years than to try ten different ways of doing the same thing. All the while many pastors seem to have no plan at all other than that of sitting down to read at random. Whatever the percentage of such persons, the seminary graduates whom I know best have not been satisfied with their ways of reading the Bible devotionally. After five years or so in the active ministry almost everyone has felt that he would attain his spiritual ideals more surely if he could follow a self-made method of reading the Bible devotionally.

The following suggestion grows out of the fact that the Bible was written by books. With an exception here and there, each book was written with the paragraph, or poetic strophe, as the literary unit. In the original, as every reader knows, only the Book of Psalms was written by chapters, and the Book of Proverbs (in the main) by verses. As for the remaining books of the English Bible, the division into chapters and verses is of comparatively modern origin. Sometimes these divisions are peculiar. Often they keep apart what God once joined together. And yet a good deal of devotional reading, even by a college and seminary graduate, may proceed with the chapter or the verse as the unit of thought.

The obvious way to deal with Holy Scripture is to take up a book at a time, and live with it for a while. Except for an occasional set of identical twins, such as the two books of Samuel, or Kings, every book unit of Holy Writ has a purpose and a character largely its own. At the university in the study of English we took up the plays of Shakespeare one at a time. Then we read each play according to its character, whether as a "history," a comedy, or a tragedy. Among the tragedies, we did not deal with *Othello* as we did with *Macbeth*. So in the Bible, no well-informed person would read the Book of Ruth the way he deals with Romans or the Revelation.

At first a good deal may depend on the choice of a Bible book. If a minister has never followed this way of reading the Bible devotionally, he may start with one of the simpler books. For example, he will find it easier to begin with Mark than with John, or with the Epistle to the Philippians than with the one to Hebrews. In time he will feel at home in these deeper waters. In devotional reading no minister should long avoid the most difficult books in the Bible, which ought to prove the most rewarding. In ten years or so a busy pastor can work his way through all these Bible books. Then he will gain far more during each successive decade of devotional reading.

Here someone may utter a protest: "Taking human nature as it is, how many of us are going to do all this devotional reading unless we can later use the harvest in feeding the flock?" The point is well taken. In devotional reading the immediate motive ought to be spiritual self-improvement. The end result, on the human level, ought to be ability to do more work and better work as a pastor, a preacher, and a pastoral leader. Here we can think only of the effect on a man's pulpit work. Let us assume that a minister determines never to preach much from a Bible book until he has lived with it long enough to know what it means as food from heaven for his own soul.

Out on the West Coast, for instance, a pastor enjoyed a yearly vacation of two months. During that time he was supposed to do a good deal of ground work for the ensuing ten months. Knowing his own tendencies he determined to read every morning straight through the Epistle to the Ephesians. This is perhaps the most difficult and sublime of Paul's Epistles. Day after day, in one version or another, starting with the Greek, he went through that letter about Christ and His Church, with its apostolic stress on the Church. Time after time, to his amazement and delight, as he strolled through those Alpine heights, he kept seeing new wonders and feeling new thrills. Afterwards he told me that never before had he enjoyed devotional readings so much as when he lived for two months with this one short letter.

During his later ministry everything seemed to be infused with the spirit of this difficult epistle. Repeatedly he went back to it for messages to the people. Like Robert William Dale at Birmingham, this other man of God could keep on preaching about the same subject, from the same Bible book, as long as his own soul continued to burn with its holy fire. In like manner, another lecturer at Yale recently told how for six months he lived with Philippians. Then he preached straight through the book, month after month, with the sort of spiritual effects that every pastor longs to see throughout the congregation.

Many a pastor feels that he ought to guide laymen in reading the Bible devotionally and helpfully. Knowing that in the morning service he can deal adequately with only four or five Bible books a year, he determines that before he begins showing the people how to read and enjoy any Bible book he will spend a number of months in reading and enjoying it himself. In this kind of personal devotions a minister can not rely on feelings that attended his Bible reading years ago. He needs to have a present experience of the blessedness that comes from living with a book inspired of God to meet human needs today.

As for the method of reading a Bible book, that will have to depend on the man. This is the way I would deal with Mark. The choice of the year's books would come during the midsummer vacation. In the fall, while preaching from Genesis, and in December a little from Micah, I would be reading daily in "The Gospel for Busy People." In Mark, as every reader knows, the trail follows the preaching of Simon Peter. The stress falls on power for service and salvation, all of it through Christ as the Son of God. In order to get a bird's-eye view of this practical Gospel, I would read it straight through at a single sitting. If the impression of the book as a whole still seemed blurred, I would read it straight through the next morning.

If necessary, I would consult a first-class Bible dictionary, or an exegetical commentary. But as a rule I would give the right of way to the book itself. Otherwise devotional reading might become an hour of study. The difference is that in devotional reading a man gives free rein to his feelings. He approaches the book in hand as a message from God to his own soul. Proceeding by paragraphs, it may be one each morning, he finds out what this unit has to show and teach him about the Christ of experience today. Before the end of the hour he has down on paper the gist of the paragraph, as it relates to the Lord Jesus, in His dealings with a Bible person or group.

In the words of the Prayer Book one ought literally to "read, mark, learn, and inwardly digest" the paragraph in hand. Into a new folder about Mark should go all of these accumulating notes about the Gospel of Christian Service (10:45). These notes a good pastoral housekeeper can preserve for the rest of his life. He can often consult them when life's trail leads him to think about the Christian use of power, over against the world's stress on selfish ends. In writing to Christians, John Mark speaks to practical folk. In reading his Gospel, any minister ought emotionally to share the experiences of those who once lived with the Christ of Galilee and Calvary.

In the ministry, as in medicine, there are two sorts of hard-working men. According to Sir William Osler, M.D., the foremost medical writer of modern times, there are in his profession those who take notes and those who do not. The man who takes notes and keeps reading continues to grow; the other does not. The one who grows follows a plan of his own devising. The other lives from hand to mouth, and often misses the connection. In other words, after a man has been in the active ministry for ten or twelve years, he ought to have within easy reach the notes from his devotional reading of all the major books in the Bible, and many of the lesser ones.

Looking for God in His Word

Any such reading calls for a certain caution. In Genesis the stress ought to fall on truth about God, always with reference to a human person, or persons. In Mark, everything ought to center round Christ. In a painting by Raphael or Michelangelo, wherever He appears, the light falls on His face. But in present-day reading of the Bible, if one may judge from devotional works in print, the stress falls mainly on human actors in the drama of redemption. At Oberammergau one summer "Judas" overshadowed "Christ," the main character. Here at home on

Good Friday "personalities round the Cross" receive much more attention than the dying Redeemer. Meanwhile, in devotional reading the power to bless still remains with Christ.

In the Book of Acts the stress ought to fall on what each paragraph tells or shows about the Living Christ, or the Holy Spirit. Whatever the passage in hand, the readings ought to proceed according to the main purpose of the Bible book. Almost every psalm has to do with God, but never apart from human experience. Into this experience a devotional reader ought to enter, day after day. From every such experience he ought to emerge with a new discovery about God. The truth that one finds may be older than the hills, but yet it comes with new joy to a reader who has just made this Bible truth his own.

As an example, take perhaps the most difficult of all the important psalms. In dealing with Ps. 139 many of us were taught to see there the omniscience and the omnipresence, the omnipotence and the transcendence of Almighty God. All of this we rejoice to believe about Him, but we wonder how any lecturer or writer could see such vast abstractions in one of the most personal and factual of all the psalms. When a person comes to it with an open mind and a needy heart he finds in it four successive lines of thought and feeling, any one of which ought to keep a person busy for an hour, reading and thinking, praying and searching his own conscience. The last main part, decidedly, is perplexing.

God knows all about me. (Vss. 1-6.)
God goes with me wherever I go. (Vss. 7-12.)
God has made me just as I am, except for
my sin. (Vss. 13-18.)
God enlists me to battle on His side. (Vss. 19-24.)

Needless to say, God-centered reading of the Psalms or of Genesis enables a minister to grow more like Him. The same holds true of Christ-centered reading in one of the Gospels, or

Spirit-centered reading in the Epistles. While the Holy Spirit and the Living Christ do not mean the same Persons, in practical enjoyment of the Acts or the Epistles a reader can never go astray if in a given book or paragraph he stresses one truth or the other. The main idea is to discover something about the Triune God, who reveals Himself in countless ways, always with reference to the needs of His children here on earth. Above all does He wish to make Himself known to a minister during hours of devotion, so that he in turn can lead others to find God through devotional reading of the Book.

Do you wish to find ways and means of enjoying morning hours of reading the Bible in the spirit of prayer? Do you likewise want to guide people into intelligent and profitable ways of reading the Bible devotionally at home? If so, why not adopt the method now in view? You will need to adapt it so as to accord with your personal needs and those of the people. But you will find the plan quite simple, at least after you get a good start. Simply by coming to know a Bible book devotionally and well, before you start sharing its treasures with others, you can keep these morning hours devotional in spirit. The later sermons will encourage lay friends to read the Bible with understanding and joy. The spirit ought to be that of the disciples on the evening of the first Easter Day:

> Did not our hearts burn within us while he talked to us on the road, while he opened to us the scriptures?
>
> —Luke 24:32 (R.S.V.)

CHAPTER IV

Intercessory Prayer

UNDER GOD THE GROWTH OF A PASTOR'S SOUL DEPENDS LARGELY on his devotional reading of the Bible in the spirit of prayer. We ought to think of these two activities as integral elements of the same transforming experience. Bible reading apart from prayer may become humanistic, and prayer without Bible reading will become impractical. On the other hand a helpful writer about things ministerial refers to a pastor's daily hour of Bible reading and prayer as "a workman's confidential interview with Him whose work he is doing, at which everything is talked over, with infinite reverence, yet frankly, with the generous Master, and instructions and assurances are received in view of fresh labours now to be attempted." [1]

Other elements enter into a minister's prayers during this morning hour of devotion. These other factors appear in the records about Hudson Taylor, founder of the China Inland Mission. Those who knew him best say that the secret of his overcoming life lay in his "daily fellowship with God." This he maintained by feeding on the Scriptures, never apart from prayer, much of it intercessory. He used to report that the hardest part of an itinerant missionary's life was to keep up regular Bible readings in the spirit of prayer. His example ought to interest a pastor who has to study in a small parsonage blessed with four lively children. How can he arrange for an early "quiet hour"?

By night at the poorest of inns Hudson Taylor would sleep in a large room filled with coolies and other transients. There

[1] See J. Oswald Dykes, *The Christian Minister and His Duties* (Edinburgh: T. & T. Clark, 1909), p. 50.

he would have a corner screened off. In the morning long before others awoke he would light his candle, read his Bible, and pray. "Take time," he would tell others. "Give God time to reveal Himself. Give yourself time to be silent before Him, waiting to receive, through the Spirit, the assurance of His presence with you, His power working in you. Take time to read His Word as in His presence, that you may know what He asks of you and what He promises you." [2]

Habits of Private Prayer

Morning after morning devotions may follow much the same course. If so, needful variety will come if the reader enters into the spirit of each Bible unit, which has a "tone color" all its own. For example, think of the difference in outlook and spiritual helpfulness between Ps. 1 and Ps. 2, or else between John 1:1-18 and the rest of the chapter. Before taking up any such passage one should ask the Spirit of God to shine upon the open page and bring the truth to light in the face of Jesus Christ. Then one can begin to read the blessed words. In the prayers that come and go during Bible reading, one need not always end with the appointed phrase, "in the name of Jesus," or anything of the sort. In prayer, however informal or brief, one ought to move in His presence, according to His character, and in a way acceptable to Him.

After a brief "prayer for illumination" one may begin to read, deliberately. If feasible, both the prayers and the readings will do their appointed work more surely if spoken aloud, with actual words, rather than with "groanings that cannot be uttered." "Take with you words, and turn to the Lord." (Hos. 14:2*a*.) If praying aloud would disturb others, then one can whisper, with voice so low that only God can hear. First of all, in reading a psalm or a parable, one may go through it as a whole, and then pray for wisdom to see it as a complete and

[2] See Dr. and Mrs. Howard Taylor, *Hudson Taylor's Spiritual Secret* (London: China Inland Mission, 1932), p. 166 *passim.*

heart-satisfying message to oneself. Later one can deal with the various parts, and ask the Lord to show what they mean in personal experience today.

For example, take the first six verses of Ps. 139. After having read the psalm as a whole, perhaps more than once, a person singles out this first main part, and then reads the six verses as a word of God to his own soul. Part by part he reads, and then he prays. "O Lord, thou hast searched me, and known me." (vs. 1.) The soul under the searchlight! The heart before the divine fluoroscope! In the *Serious Call* William Law says that if the world knew a man as the Lord knows him, and as he ought to know himself, he would not receive admiration and honor because of any supposed goodness and wisdom. In like manner Dwight L. Moody used to say that a man's religion means what he is in the dark when alone with his God. For some such reasons Mark Twain is said to have dreaded being alone at night.

During such a give-and-take interview with his Lord, how should a minister feel? Much as young Isaiah felt when he beheld a vision of God's holiness (Isa. 8:1-8). Such a feeling of awe may lead to a few brief, faltering words of adoration, and then to a sentence or two of confession. Confession first for his own sins, as they appear under God's searchlight. Confession also for the sins of others whom he loves. In private devotions a man's prayers normally start with himself. No matter what the Bible passage in hand, it has some bearing on his own heart and life. Prayers for self may continue until he comes out into the sunshine of God's favor. After a renewed assurance of reasons for inner peace, there comes a need of prayers for others. Intercessions may follow in everwidening circles, as in Ps. 103, though that is not a prayer.

Beginning with oneself and God, where religion always begins, a prayer may follow an old-time pattern, but not slavishly. Using a familiar acrostic, one may think of ACTSS. This means Adoration—Confession—Thanksgiving—Supplication (which includes petitions for loved ones in the home and intercessions for others elsewhere)—and Submission (which may concern sanctification, service, or acceptance of suffering). Such an account may seem formal, stiff, and wooden. Even so, if from day to day one of these five elements does not enter prominently into a man's prayers, something vital may be missing from his soul. Within such a general framework "the effectual prayer of a righteous man" tends to be personal and factual. Like Ps. 139 and many another Bible outpouring of a heart before God, a minister's private prayers may well abound in facts, facts, facts, all of them about persons, human and divine.

During the early part of a devotional hour a person may remain seated at his desk, before the open Bible. At times he may simply bow his head and with eyes closed talk things over with his Lord. But sometime toward the end he should kneel. David Livingstone wrote in his Journal at the age of thirty-nine that he had long made it a habit to "approach God in secret with as much reverence as in public." According to our ablest book on the psychology of religion, "The external aids to prayer, the bent knee, the closed eyes, and other postures commonly used in worship have on the worshiper a decidedly helpful effect in bringing about a religious attitude of mind." [3] On the contrary, a young pastor suffered spiritual loss by following the suggestion of an older clergyman who said that he held his evening devotions in bed. With him there may have been a physical reason; for the younger man there was no earthly excuse. If private devotions become easy, or soporific, they lose their spiritual value.

For some such reasons a certain pastor reserves in the study a prayer nook. Another has a special chair. A third, not at all "high church," has a *prie-dieu* (a stool with a summons to "pray God"). By way of starting a current of devotion in the soul when sluggish, more than one minister has at hand a book of

[3] See James B. Pratt, *The Religious Consciousness* (New York: Macmillan Co., 1928), p. 314.

prayers by other men. Many of us find it helpful to read only the Bible, with an occasional dip into a hymnal. After a period of reading any vital part of Holy Writ, a man who loves the Lord should be ready to pray.

Prayer of the right sort always costs. Sometimes people sing about the "beautiful garden of prayer," as though it meant enjoying the serenity of moonlight and the fragrance of roses. In the Garden of Gethsemane the prayers of our Lord caused Him to sweat as it were great drops of blood. Hence George Adam Smith wrote about private prayer as a battlefield, a phrase that others have borrowed:

> Our Lord not only made prayer the battlefield of life, but when victory came He followed it up with renewed prayer and communion with His Father. Every fresh achievement of power He made a fresh occasion for enlistment to the struggle before Him. Every summit to which His Father lifted Him He used as an altar for another consecration of Himself to the Father's service.[4]

Resourcefulness in Prayer

From the lives of good men anyone can learn much about ways of private devotion. In the long run, however, each minister has to do his own praying, and in his own manner. On such a private battlefield why should any young David sally forth clad in the armor of some older King Saul? Wise counsel here comes from a liberal evangelical of yesterday, Charles E. Jefferson:

> Be entirely yourself. If you are genuinely yourself you will not pray like anybody else. . . . Begin by speaking the thing uppermost in your heart. Always start where you are. Let your present experience determine what you are to say first. If you are full of gratitude, give thanks. If you are weighed down with contrition, confess your

[4] See *The Forgiveness of Sins and Other Sermons* (New York: Eaton & Mains, 1905), p. 85.

sins. If you earnestly desire some particular thing, pray for it at once. If it is not your own need but the need of others that is most potent in your thought, let your prayer begin with intercession. Much depends on beginning aright. You do not begin right unless you begin where you are most alive.[5]

Amen, especially if a man has just read a Bible message from God to himself. As the years go by he will note that whenever the tides have risen highest in his soul he has tended to pray largely for others. Without neglecting any other element necessary to the completeness of private prayers, he may give special prominence to thanksgiving and to intercession, especially the latter. If like John Wesley a pastor looks on the world as his parish, he will pray for the world dear to the heart of God. If he thinks more often in terms of the local church and community, he will pray for others there, but he will never lose sight of the fact that the home congregation is an integral part of the Holy Catholic Church. On the contrary, if private prayers become personal, parochial, and provincial, the Lord may soon permit leanness to come into that soul.

Whatever their nature at a given time, private prayers ought as a rule to be specific and factual. Instead of vaguely imploring the Lord to bless "all the members of this congregation," and "all the missionaries in Africa," a man does better to single out a certain type of person, age group, or mission station, and then ask the Lord for a specific blessing that the facts call for. One summer in a rural parsonage of North Carolina a pastor lay abed week after week, recovering from typhoid fever. Every day in prayer he made the rounds of that community, interceding by name for every man, woman, or child, regardless of race, color, or church membership. Each time he asked the Lord to do for an unseen friend what his soul needed most. In the fall the minister discovered that while he had lain abed and en-

[5] See Charles E. Jefferson, "How to Pray," a leaflet, n.d.

gaged in prayer for others the tides of spiritual life throughout the community had risen higher than ever before. All the while in their homes the people had kept praying for their beloved leader.

In the study of a certain church the pastor has a sort of rotary wheel. On it he has cards with the names of the members, arranged by districts, and according to families alphabetically. Every morning he plans to go through the cards of friends in a certain district. Thus he can visit with all the church members, one after another, by way of the mercy seat. Much the same plan lends itself to prayer for missionary friends overseas. Many of them the pastor has never seen. Still he should rejoice to believe in "the communion of saints."

Any such discussion can at best be only suggestive—not exhaustive. If the testimony has come largely from other men, the reason is that they not only believed in prayer; they prayed. In the light of their experiences we may conclude that the vitality of a minister's private prayers depends largely on the reality and the scope of his intercessions for others, both near and far. In his *Table Talk* Martin Luther refers to such prayers as a "climbing of the heart up to God." Surely this ought to mean sharing His concern for "the world and the individual," according to their spiritual needs just now.

"But what if my mind wanders?" Being human, every person has such experiences. The ablest man I have ever known, in the way of practical intelligence, once said publicly that he had never been able to keep his attention fixed on one thing for more than three minutes at a time. He was a praying man and no doubt he often let his mind wander during daily devotions. If so, why not pray about the person or thing to which the mind turns? That may be the very person or thing about which the Lord wishes a minister to intercede. Whatever comes welling up from unconscious depths may need cleansing from the Lord, who knows all about that hidden slime.

If a man's prayers keep following his wandering thoughts the time of devotion may seem disjointed. But so does the talk of a little boy who keeps telling his father whatever pops into the little fellow's mind. Strange as it may seem, the Heavenly Father enjoys informality and frankness. For evidence read the prayers of a saint in the central part of Jeremiah. But still such discursiveness may go too far. As a partial safeguard more than one pastor follows the habit of praying aloud. Such a man may feel that private prayer is too "secret," so he brings his prayers out into the open, and puts them into audible words. Still another minister uses his pen. Somehow or other, morning after morning, he writes out a brief prayer. Whenever a man prays, whatever the method, he should listen to God, talk to God, and meditate about God, about anything that concerns God, himself, and others.

Prayer at Other Times

After an hour of devotion a minister continues to pray throughout the morning and the rest of the day. When Paul wrote the first of his "letters to young churches," he enjoined the brethren to "pray without ceasing" (I Thess. 5:17). He must have been referring to his own custom, and holding it up as an example for the local pastor and his people. Such unscheduled petitions the fathers used to call "ejaculatory," a term that suggests the spasmodic, or the explosive. In lieu of a more exact term let us call these bits of quiet conversation with the unseen One "informal prayers." In the preparation of a sermon, in making ready for midweek worship, or in any part of a morning's work, why not keep in touch with headquarters?

The same idea works equally well throughout the afternoon and evening. In counseling with a husband and wife on the verge of a divorce, in calling on the sick, in waiting at a door when the other person seems not to be at home, often a minister senses the need of wisdom higher than his own. Even if there be nothing in the way of perplexity, still the people who live on the other side of that closed door need the minister's prayers. Indeed, some of them may attach to his prayers more importance than he seems to. Why else do they come to him at times and ask him to pray for a loved one?

A pastor of the right sort becomes known as a man of prayer (Cf. I Sam. 12:19-24, especially vs. 23). When he goes into certain homes the people ask him to read from the Book and offer prayer. If they do not, as a rule he asks for the privilege. At least this used to be the case more than it seems to have been of late, when people have more pressing needs than ever. In a household where the elderly father was a paralytic a visitor inquired about the minister's prayers. The wife replied: "He never does anything but tell jokes, sometimes the same old chestnuts." "Why don't you invite him to pray?" "Oh, I did not know that it was proper to do that any more!" Such cases are more common than an outsider would suppose.

Near Princeton, New Jersey, the eight Protestant ministers of a rural district became concerned about the low estate of community religion and morals. One day they met to consider ways and means of bringing about a local revival. Of course they began to think about importing a professional evangelist. One of the pastors remarked that even if they could secure the right sort of leader from outside, still there was need of preliminary spade work at home. Soon those men discovered that only one of the group ever had family prayers in his home. With such a prayerless beginning at home who can wonder that throughout the day a clergyman muddles through many a mess without once looking up for guidance?

Herein may lie the chief cause of a pastor's failure to keep growing. Hudson Taylor used to declare, "A minister can work without praying, but he can not pray without working." In our Lord's reported utterances He said more about prayer than about preaching. Here we need not think about a minister's prayers in public,[6] at a committee meeting, or before he

[6] See my *Leading in Public Prayer* (Nashville: Abingdon Press, 1958).

answers a provocative letter. If he finds that he does not feel like praying at any such time of need, perhaps he has never really learned how to pray. Indeed, many of us have made a like discovery. Fortunately, a person can learn to pray by praying under the guiding hand of the Holy Spirit.

God ever stands ready to do His full share, and more. If through the day, the week, and the year a minister prays aright, especially for others, the Lord will deal bountifully with his servant. But he must continually rely on God. "I feel the need of trusting Him here as well as in other matters. We must get our prayers from God." So spake a Christlike missionary, Fraser of Isuland. To his remark let us add a phrase from the Prayer Book: "We must get our prayers from God," "from whom cometh every good prayer." A long while ago (1729) William Law summed up the whole matter about a man's private devotions:

> Devotion is . . . a life given to God. He is the devout man, therefore, who considers and serves God in everything and who makes all of life an act of devotion by doing everything in the name of God and under such rules as are conformable to His glory.[7]

[7] See *A Serious Call to a Devout and Holy Life,* ed. by John W. Meister, *et al.* (Philadelphia: Westminster Press, 1955), p. 17.

CHAPTER V

Intellectual Labor

WE HAVE BEEN THINKING ABOUT BIBLE READING AND PRAYER AS the food and the atmosphere essential to the growth of a pastor's soul. Along with these ways of spiritual self-development we ought to include intellectual labor. Day after day hard work ought to serve as the norm, both in morning study and during later hours. Otherwise a graduate of college and seminary may cease to seem educated for his calling. At least on the surface—where most laymen live, or survive—the needs and the problems of human beings have largely changed in the past ten years, and they bid fair to change much more in the next decade. Does the pastor keep up with his times?

On the other hand, hard work with the brain tends to insure the right sort of growth:

> Not only does the ministerial calling require eminent piety, but it tends to produce it. . . . A man is unconsciously molded by his daily routine of duties. . . . Hence a faithful performance of clerical duties contributes directly to spirituality. . . . Study—close, persevering study—improves his religious character. . . . The mind must do something. If it is not occupied with great and good themes, it will be busy with small and frivolous ones. . . . The holiest men in the Christian Church have been the most studious.[1]

This excerpt comes from an able book by a professor of systematic theology, As examples of ministers who kept on growing spiritually because of unremitting intellectual toil this old-time professor singled out John Calvin and Richard Baxter.

[1] See Wm. G. T. Shedd, *Homiletics and Pastoral Theology* (New York: Charles Scribner's Sons, 1867), pp. 283-86.

Between Calvin's twenty-seventh year, when he sent out the first edition of the *Institutes,* and his fifty-fifth, when he went home to his God, he kept maturing, not least in his emotions. For part of the evidence turn to his letters, which have been published. As for Richard Baxter, the professor just quoted advised young ministers to read the *Reformed Pastor* at least once a year. Neither Baxter nor Calvin enjoyed good health, but each of them did an amazing amount of intellectual labor. For instance, take Baxter's devotional classic, *The Saint's Everlasting Rest.* In like manner study John Wesley and his intellectual labors throughout a lifetime of strenuous activity.

Another example comes from America. In recent years scholars at Yale and elsewhere have rediscovered Jonathan Edwards, who was born in 1703, the same year as John Wesley. Unfortunately, Edwards has been known chiefly through a single discourse, "Sinners in the Hands of an Angry God,"—which was published in 1741,—not through his ablest writings, all of which came after he was ejected from his parish in 1750. Between that time and his demise early in 1758, he kept on growing in likeness to the One who is said to have been made "perfect through sufferings" (Heb. 2:10*c*). Thank God for these and all other apostles of hard intellectual labor!

Labor in the Pastor's Study

In each case mentioned above, the labor had to do largely with the Bible and books about the Bible. Every one of those men had a competent knowledge of the book learning in his time. But still in a way much his own, each of them became a master of this one Book. Even for a man with unusual powers, such a mastery comes only through exacting toil, spread out over years. Not content with devotional readings early in the day, the local interpreter of God's holy Book needs later to delve into it with all his mental powers, and with the best available tools in the way of exegetical commentaries and other scholarly works. Once formed, such habits of intellectual toil continue to bring delight through the years. But, alas, so does the current fashion of spending hours watching television tend to persist. Eternity alone will show much pastoral dereliction of intellectual duty has been due to overindulgence in enjoyment of light entertainment over television, and of other frivolous things not wrong in themselves. Today, more than ever before, such things tend to keep a man from his books and his prayers.

Especially in the early years of the ministry a pastor has to work hard on his sermons. If he knows Hebrew and Greek, especially the latter, his labors ought to begin there. Apart from more practical benefits, any man who has learned how to use either "dead" language has for once in his life done hard intellectual work. If he has done it well, he has learned what the fathers meant by "the gospel of work," and the joy of difficult achievement. He ought also to know Latin, German, and French, at least well enough to read the New Testament in any of those tongues. With a mastery of such tools, and the guidance of scholars through books, anyone can learn to find joy in preparing to preach.

That joy will come more surely if a man forms the habit of not bypassing difficult parts of Holy Writ. While he is learning to handle his tools he may content himself with setting forth obvious truths in easy psalms, parables, and epistles. In Philippians, for instance, he may encounter few obstacles, except in the paragraph about the present-day meaning of the Incarnation (2:5-11). Among countless other advantages of mastering the Bible a book at a time, and then preaching one's way here and there through the book one has recently mastered, not least is this: one dares to preach about the most important passages, however difficult. Needless to say, in a single discourse no one can exhaust this paragraph about the Incarnation, or this subject. But if the first message of the sort is to be clear and interesting, practical and helpful, while true to the facts of revelation and life, the man in the study must toil in the spirit of prayer.

Thus far we have been thinking about work in preparing a sermon more or less expository. At least for the sake of variety in pulpit fare, there is need also of doctrinal sermons, and ethical ones, not specially expository. If a man is fortunate enough to have two services on the Lord's Day, and one in the middle of the week, he can at the "eleven-o'clock hour" have a popular and inspiring message that nobody but himself will label as "expository." Then at the "second service," a doctrinal sermon, or an ethical one, tópical in form, and Biblical in substance. The latter may be the harder to prepare, and the more helpful to the hearer.

A wise man says that during the week no two services ought to meet the same sort of needs, or have the same spirit and form. In other words, strive for variety of purpose, of content, and of form, especially this last. In the middle of the week, for example, a pastor may guide lay friends in reading and enjoying a book of the Bible, far removed from the one he is using in sermons on the Lord's Day. As for details, every man should work them out for himself. One thing seems sure: if a man does such pulpit work at all well, week after week, he must toil tremendously. Also, he must have time for uninterrupted study, and thereby he will grow spiritually.

The basic idea is that a pastor should arrange the year's pulpit work so as to require the daily use of all his intellectual powers and resources. For the first year or two, while he is acquiring tools to handle, and learning how to use them expertly, a seminary graduate may thank God if he has only a single message to prepare each week, it may be as an assistant pastor. But how any mature clergyman can remain content with only one hour of public worship a week is a mystery to me. Except when he has a circuit of small churches he ought to know that people in the community need more than one opportunity for worship. This ought to include a message that may have "come out of great tribulation," in the form of intellectual travail.

Personally, I did most of my doctrinal and ethical preaching at night. Incidentally, as a pastor I did not preach at night to empty pews. I know that with each passing decade it has become more difficult to secure a respectable number of hearers at night. I also know that the need for more than one hour of worship has increased with each passing decade. If anyone asks why the Roman Church is forging ahead here in the States, one answer is that the hours of stated worship accord with the varieties of human nature among the laity, not merely with the convenience of the leaders in worship. In as far as I can see and judge, if local Protestantism contents itself with a one-hour-a-week schedule for the public worship of God, our part of the Church will be on the way out.

On the other hand, nothing in the laws of God or man ordains that the "second service" must come after dark. If that time does not suit the convenience or the desires of those who ought to come, why not shift to a more acceptable hour? If so, the "second service"—whether it be at 8:30 A.M. or at 5:00 P.M.—need not be "identical" with the one at 11:00 A.M. Remember that working rule: during any week no two hours of public worship with the same purpose and of the same character. For example, with two hours of stated worship on the Lord's Day a minister can think of one in terms of attracting young folk, with boys and girls, and others who do not as yet feel the need of instructive preaching.

Then at the other service he can deliberately set himself to teach, and that attractively. After a protracted course of reading in standard books he can prepare a number of sermons about the "Incarnation," the "Atonement," "the Resurrection," "The Living Christ," or "what our Lord says about the hereafter." On none of these vast subjects can a single sermon do much more than open up the subject. But if a person is to prepare a succession of messages about any of these doctrines, he must read and think and pray. "What does Holy Scripture teach on this subject, or on that? What does it mean, for instance, to have the Holy Spirit as our Teacher? How can I make this truth clear, luminous, and effective in the heart and life of the hearer?" Work!

The answers come through intellectual toil, and that during a period of weeks and months!

Labor with Scholarly Books

In order to do hard intellectual work a pastor needs to have scholarly books. Among them think of standard exegetical commentaries. This refers to books of exegesis and exposition, leaving every minister the joy of working out his own homiletics. Exegesis preferably starts with the Greek or the Hebrew. In the light of the Bible book and its purpose the exegete deals with each passage in detail. Exposition takes these facts of exegesis and puts them together in a helpful synthesis. Exegesis has to do with painstaking analysis; exposition, with equally careful synthesis, which calls for the use of imagination as the synthesizing power.

The difference between exegesis and exposition appears in well-known sets, which always prove unequal in value. In the *International Critical Commentary,* the volume on Romans, by Sanday and Headlam, is perhaps the best of many scholarly treatments of that major epistle. In the same series the volume about Samuel seems to me not worth its shelf room. Other exegetical work of a high order appears in many parts of the current *Interpreter's Bible,* most of it by liberal evangelicals, and in the older *Expositor's Greek Testament,* as well as in such old-time standbys as the sets by Meyer and by Lange. As for popular expository work it appears at the foot of the page in many parts of *The Interpreter's Bible.* For many such reasons, in addition to a standard set or two, many of us prefer to single out the best available treatment of each Bible book. Incidentally, it takes almost as much brains and care to select a commentary as to use it.

The same principle applies to the choice of other books. For easy reference a man needs a first-class encyclopedia, such as the *Encyclopedia Britannica.* He also needs an unabridged English dictionary, a world atlas, and a current issue of the

World Almanac. To these one should add a standard Bible dictionary or two, a full-size concordance, and other works of reference as the need arises. Among them all I get help especially from the *Dictionary of Christ and the Gospels,* and the *Dictionary of the Apostolic Church,* each in two volumes, and edited by James Hastings, not all of whose "preacher's helps" merit commendation.

A pastor's library ought to be worthy of note for quality rather than size. Among commentaries, books of reference, works on theology, or anything else, why should he give shelf room to anything but the best? As for the best, there are two guides, both of them excellent. First, that of expert opinion. Which commentaries rank highest with masters in a particular field? For instance, a man needs for speedy reference a single-volume commentary. Many conservatives agree with experts at Union Seminary, Richmond, in recommending two such Lutheran volumes, one on the Old Testament, edited by Allemann and Flack; the other on the New, by Flack. Personally, I often use these "liberal evangelical" one-volume commentaries: the *Abingdon,* and the *New Commentary,* edited by Gore; and the conservative British *New Bible Commentary,* edited by F. Davidson and others.

The second dependable guide is that of practical use. Experience quickly shows that what delights an erudite seminary professor may not fit the intellectual needs and limitations of a certain pastor. Partly for this reason the sizing up of books ought to start early in a man's first year of seminary work, and continue beyond graduation day. With the new diploma a graduate of a divinity school ought to carry away something equally precious: a list of scholarly commentaries, and of other learned books, each of which he has used often enough and long enough to know that it is worth his buying and using the rest of his life.

Especially in the field of theology a minister needs standard books. He may leave to lay preachers the buying and the use of works intended to make life in the study easy. At least mentally every pastor needs a private *index expurgatorius.* On it he may put digests, compendiums, and other handiwork of men who have combed the original sources and extracted much honey. On the proscribed list some of us put the *Pulpit Commentary,* the *Biblical Illustrator,* books of canned illustrations, and other kinds of ministerial "cake-mix" devised to keep young clergymen from employing their brains. Like the poor these books are ever with us. Often they prove helpful, however, to a lay preacher who has had no training in the use of books, and who has no time to prepare homemade sermons.

A pastor ought to enjoy his hours in the study, and not merely endure them. Enjoyment never comes through relying on predigested pap for immature preachers. At first it may seem impossible to pay for a first-class working library. But if a man singles out a few Bible books for mastery each year, and a number of basic doctrines to study, he can stock up on standard literature about these parts of Scripture and of theology. In ten years he can own a good working library. As for the other books, at nominal cost for postage a minister can secure worthy volumes through applying to the library of any first-class seminary. With some exceptions, standard books from yesterday are not usually in demand. On the basis of such reading in borrowed books, a pastor can keep adding to the list of ones for future purchase. In short, a minister can be judged fairly well by the number and character of the books in his library.

Labor to Keep Educated

A wise observer of men describes an educated man as one who is able to converse intelligently with the widest variety of people, each time on a subject of vital concern to the other person. From this point of view every pastor faces the question of how to keep educated. In our calling a man needs to be well read and well informed, especially about his own field. In a single week he may be asked about the Dead Sea Scrolls and their relation to the Essenes; or the reason for a certain attitude toward

Billy Graham, Norman Vincent Peale, Paul Tillich, one of the Niebuhr brothers, Karl Barth, Emil Brunner, Martin Buber, or Sören Kierkegaard. If a minister was graduated ten years ago, and has not read much since, he cannot make a stagger at most of the answers. Surely laymen have a right to expect their pastor to be intelligently informed about leading religious personages and issues in our day.

With each passing year new personalities and issues will emerge. As in the Wonderland of childhood days, life moves swiftly today. In other times, to paraphrase young Alice—you got somewhere if you ran very fast for a long time. But now it seems, as the Queen told Alice, "It takes all the running you can do to keep in the same place." In other words, nobody can hope to know the answers to all the questions that come to a minister. For example, a pastor may not be able to answer a question about the meaning of Einstein's theory of relativity. Surely no one wishes his minister to seem "superficially omniscient." If he does not know, he ought to be frank, and not hazard a guess. If the matter seems important, he should look it up.

In talking with a woman who knows much about Missions a pastor ought to know the geography of the Middle East and of Africa. He should know that the map of the world has changed since he was in grade school, and that Ghana is not a river in Siberia. So with the tenets of Muslims, the appeal of Buddhists to some of our intelligentsia, and the reasons for the rapid spread of Protestantism in Brazil, but not in Argentina. Again, friendly talk with a "lay reader" may concern the proper attitude toward Jehovah's Witnesses, or the congency of what Reinhold Niebuhr has written of late about the unwisdom of trying to win converts from Judaism.

About the importance of such questions opinions may differ. I have been writing out of my own recent experiences while in charge of a suburban church. One purpose of this chapter is to raise questions to which a reader, or reviewer, will give answers not suggested here. But let us agree that in every community a pastor ought to take his place in the forefront of those who read and think, largely in thought forms of today. Ten years from now, let us hope, he will be abreast of his new times.

A regime of this sort requires much reading, all of it self-regulated. The schedule permits limited time for the local newspaper, and more time relatively for such magazines as *Harper's,* the *Atlantic Monthly,* and the *Saturday Review*. The idea is, when feasible, to read only what is well written. According to John Oman of Cambridge University, a shrewd observer, the chief weakness of many clergymen lies in comparative ignorance of great books, even in their own tongue. Among living authors, for instance, a minister ought to know the works of T. S. Eliot, especially *The Waste Land* (1922) and *Murder in the Cathedral* (1935).

As for current fiction every pastor knows two books by Alan Paton, who always writes well: *Cry, the Beloved Country* (1948) and *Too Late the Phalarope* (1953). A minister ought also to know three novels by Albert Camus: *The Plague* (1948), *The Stranger* (1956), and *The Fall* (1957). With respect to most current fiction, I have often browsed among novels lauded by gifted reviewers. Now I welcome the counsel of Douglas Bush, professor of English at Harvard. He advises readers to leave current novels largely alone, and to prefer biography, in which recent authors have excelled. About any such deliverance professors at Princeton or Yale might shake their heads in dissent.

If there were time, I should add something about the wisdom of preserving the best of what one has read. But I have discussed that elsewhere.[2] As an example of the way the business works, take this that I once read in a first-class mystery story, but did not write down. How I wish I had in store the fruits of wide and varied reading in those prodigal days when I did not keep notes! More recently I came across the very same words quoted in an-

[2] See *Planning a Year's Pulpit Work,* Appendix, "Storing the Fruits of Study" (Nashville: Abingdon Press, 1942).

other book. This time I wrote them out and put them in a folder. Hence I can recall them and use them here to sum up what we have been thinking about a pastor's need of intellectual labor for the sake of his own soul:

> A man's brain, originally, is like a little empty attic, and you have to stock it with such furniture as you choose. A fool takes in all the lumber of every sort that he comes across, so that the knowledge which might be useful to him is crowded out, or at best is jumbled up with a lot of other things, so that he has difficulty in laying his hands upon it. Now the skilled workman is very careful indeed about what he takes into his brain-attic. He will have nothing but the tools which may help him in doing his work, but of these he has a large assortment, and all in the most perfect order.[3]

[3] See Christopher Morley, ed., *Sherlock Holmes and Mr. Watson* (New York: Harcourt, Brace & Co., 1944), p. 16.

CHAPTER VI

Pastoral Activity

LET US NOW CONSIDER PASTORAL ACTIVITY AS A GOD-GIVEN MEANS of grace. Later we shall think about the minister as leader of the congregation as a whole and its broader activities. Here we can deal only with what he does for people in their homes, and with them one by one in his study. This kind of activity calls for time, skill, patience, and heart power. In all of this activity a pastor works for others, rather than himself. Here again we must distinguish between unselfish motives and the most assured rewards. According to the laws of God, whenever a man uses aright his gifts of love and compassion, these gifts from God increase.

Pastoral Counseling

In ministerial circles today the stress often falls on counseling with persons in need, and as a rule, one at a time. In dealing with husband and wife, temporarily estranged, a pastor may confer with them separately, and then bring them together. Whenever a minister prays for others publicly, or preaches the Gospel, he makes clear whether or not he is the kind of person to whom one can come for understanding, sympathy, and help, "without money and without price." As a matter of fact, after he learns what the Lord wishes him to do in the pulpit he often engages in pastoral counseling there, as a sort of God-given preventive medicine. Especially in summer, when disorders of the soul often abound, an up-to-date pastor may deal with a number of appropriate psalms about anxiety, insecurity, despondency, and guilt.

Such messages do a pastor good. But woe be to his people if

that is the reason for his preaching. Recently when asked to take part in a Good Friday service, a student of divinity replied: "That will be good training for me." If so, that was his reward. But when a counselor forgets about himself and his lavish expenditure of time on what may seem like a hopeless case, the Lord blesses this use of spiritual muscles. Sometimes an outsider wonders why people love their minister so much, and why he has become such a good man. The answer may lie in his quiet work as a counselor.

The counselor blessed of God looks on his friend across the table as a person, not merely a case. The resulting interview, ideally, increases the pastor's knowledge of human nature, his patience in listening without interruption, his insight into the depths of other souls, his refusal to seem shocked by evidences of sin and shame hidden beneath the surface, and his skill in leading the other person out into the sunshine of God's favor. Simply by going over this list, which is not complete, anyone can see that these qualities are inseparable parts of Christlike character.

One other virtue may follow, that of humility. Some of the men who write about such things appear to cure all their cases, often during a single interview. My friends in the medical world do not count a case of skin cancer cured until after a lapse of five years. Except in a city where a clergyman often deals with transients, a pastor can see whether or not the alcoholic husband and wife continue to remain sober, and whether the reconciled husband and wife "live happily ever after." Every such failure, or imperfect piece of work, sends a pastor to his knees, there to confess his lack of wisdom, and to seek God's blessing on him as a counselor of souls.

All the while, if he perseveres, he will grow more and more like the Ideal Counselor. For example, take what the apostle Paul writes about the fruit of the Spirit: "love, joy, peace, patience, kindness, goodness, faithfulness, gentleness, and self-control" (Gal. 5:22). How can a young minister hope to attain such Christlike qualities? Not by thinking about them abstractly, and not by striving after them desperately. No, not by agonizing efforts, but by welcoming every opportunity to exercise these graces in dealing with human beings, preferably one at a time. Even if occasionally he seems to fail, so did our Lord "fail" with the rich young ruler. Every such hour of counseling affords an opportunity to grow:

> The trivial round, the common task,
> Will give [me] all [I] ought to ask;
> Room to deny [myself], a road
> To bring [me] daily nearer God.

Pastoral Calling

The same truth applies to pastoral visitation. Even if the minister's calls on the sick, the distressed, and the people in general did little or nothing for other persons concerned, such activity would seem necessary for the growth of a man's soul. This may be partly why it is easier for a minister to be Christlike while he is a pastor than when he engages in teaching, or in full-time administrative work. According to Dame Rumor a young lad with more zeal than tact went up to an elderly stranger with a long white beard and accosted him with a question: "Are you a Christian?" "Sir," said the venerable gentleman, "I would have you know that I am a theological professor!" "Well," replied the young fellow, "if I were you, I shouldn't let that keep me from being a Christian!" No, of course not, ideally! But what are the facts? Here I must plead some sort of Fifth Amendment, lest the facts incriminate me.

Because of changing conditions in every community and its homes, pastoral oversight worthy of the name grows more difficult from year to year. In fact, it never was free from difficulty. For seventeen years I enjoyed such activities. Then for long years as a teacher I could not deal much with church people, except on the Lord's Day from the pulpit. During recent years

I have served as interim pastor, in one field after another. Month by month when calling I have encountered obstacles largely unknown in those earlier years. But I have also found increasing personal satisfaction. In as far as I have been able to judge, I have accomplished more of late by going to homes than in any other way. To take an example from the present field, after I began to do systematic calling, the attendance at public worship and prayer meeting began to increase. So it still seems to be true that "a house-going pastor means a church-going people." Lack of regular attendance by members and officers is the most serious problem of Protestant churches.

If I were a full-time pastor I should give careful attention to plans for this part of the work. A man ought not to do it the same way as his grandfather who drove a Model T Ford. But in as far as I can see and learn, there is in almost every congregation much more need of pastoral oversight now than there was in former decades. Many families have moved, and still feel uprooted. Many more church members are contemplating divorce. Modern inventions have largely done away with old-time customs of "neighboring." In home after home there is a sense of lostness and a need of personal guidance. As any home-going pastor could report, the need is for someone who knows, who cares, and who is able to guide toward the Lord.

Once again, what does it mean to excel as a pastor? If only to secure emphasis by repetition, let the answer come from Paul. In well-known words about the greatness of Christlike love, he has left us a word picture of a saint, a man who has grown saintly by serving as a pastor. In the following list of sixteen Christian graces, see if there is one that does not increase through diligent exercise in the routine of pastoral calling. From this point of view let me paraphrase a little:

A Christlike pastor suffers long and is kind. He envies not, vaunts not himself, is not puffed up, does not behave himself unseemly, seeks not his own, is not easily provoked, thinks no evil; rejoices not in iniquity, but rejoices in the truth; bears all things, believes all things, hopes all things, endures all things. The love of a good pastor never fails.

Sick Visitation

A man with a shepherd heart comes into his own when he cares for the sick. The illness may be in the body, in the mind, or in both. Whatever the nature and the seriousness of a malady, he stands ready to help. Whether the patient recovers or not, the minister never ceases to be dear to the household. The members look to him as the physician of their souls. Usually we think that he can render these services because he is a good man. That of course is correct. But anyone who watches him from year to year can see that he is becoming a better man. With a pastor as with a physician, daily contact with persons in distress tends to make a man better or worse.

A minister of the right sort can rise to an emergency. A long-awaited baby is still-born. Another one is born a blue baby, a spectacle pitiful to behold. A full-grown daughter goes to the hospital with an unbalanced mind, and probably she will never again see her home. An only son far away in the Air Corps crashes in his plane. A loved one takes his own life. Into such a family circle comes a man of God. With no magic word or mystic spell he sits in silence and causes everyone to feel that the Lord is here, that He knows, that He cares, and that He can bless these breaking hearts. Out from every such experience a pastor should emerge a better man.

In dealing with certain shut-in saints a minister can receive far more than he has to give. Late on Saturday afternoon, alone with an aged friend in a modest upper room, a pastor may feel that for him "this is the house of God, and this is the gate of heaven." With a verse from the Psalms, or part of an old-time hymn, the guest can start a stream of quiet talk. Simply by listening he can learn what it means to live with God here and now, while waiting for the sound of the trumpet from the other side of the river. Among all the experiences to which a former pastor looks back, none help him more than these memories of "quiet seasons in the soul." "By these things do men live," and thus become Godlike.

Personal Evangelism

A growing minister feels increasing concern about the unsaved and the unchurched in the local community. The discussion here relates only to what he himself does in what Bishop Roy Short of The Methodist Church calls "the salvaging of souls," one by one. In "the days of His flesh" our Lord devoted much of His time and strength to "individual work with the individual." Anyone who would grow like Him needs to do the same. Much of this man-to-man work he cannot delegate. Whenever feasible the pastor enlists the help of a dedicated layman or woman. But with some persons the minister himself should represent his Lord.

Does such a minister engage in personal work because he is good, or does he become good by engaging in personal work? Surely the matter works both ways. In Scotland a village pastor had the reputation of speaking to every person in the community about the welfare of his soul. On our side of the water the minister of a large church made it a rule not to introduce for church membership any candidate with whom he had not held a personal interview or two. In each case the minister became known as a man of God, and through the years people said that he became more and more like his Lord. In other words, God blesses the right sort of ministerial soul winning.

In Dallas when I knew George W. Truett he had the oversight of a church of eight thousand members and a vast plant. He had drawn about him a staff of experts, and a host of lay workers, but he never ceased to bear on his heart the welfare of sinners and worldlings, one by one. At an evening service he once preached about prayer. The next day on the street he met a well-known lawyer, not at all a Christian. The lawyer referred to the sermon, which he had heard. Then he asked if the minister ever prayed for an unbelieving lawyer. Truett reached into his pocket, took out a notebook, and showed the lawyer his own name, with the assurance that for a number of years the pastor had been praying for him by name. Do you wonder that with all of his attainments and achievements, Truett impressed me most by his saintliness? He had kept growing through spiritual exercise.

Fortunately, a minister need not be a saint before he starts doing personal work. In as far as I have been able to estimate the ways in which the Lord most blessed me as a young pastor, I feel that He did so when I was not thinking about my own spiritual pulse, but when I was intent on introducing a needy person to Christ. In those earlier years I sometimes had questions about matters of belief and practice. For a time I did not feel sure about "the resurrection of the body," and about certain aspects of Christian duty. But afterwards I could see that those questions did not arise when I was showing concern about the unsaved and the unchurched. At such times of "greater visibility" matters of doctrine and duty have a way of falling into line with the truths of revelation and the needs of the busy toiler.

To be sure, the current ways of church work may keep a minister so busy attending meetings and working on committees that he has little time and energy left for personal work. One time long ago we pastors were engaged in a city-wide movement for evangelism. Every Monday we held an all-day conference at a hotel, with a midday meal that some of us could scarcely afford, or swallow, because our wives were at home busy with babies and the week's washing. Hour after hour we listened to far-sighted plans by skyscraper experts who knew and cared little about local conditions and needs. One afternoon my head began to feel dizzy with trying to figure out the connection between vast paper schemes and winning a lost soul in our part of the city.

Then I stole out of the meeting and started home. On the way I stopped to see a woman with a non-American background, on whom I had been too busy to call. Alone in a strange country and city, she and her husband had been trying to grope their way toward God. After that call, and another one later when her husband was at home, with the co-operation of lay friends in the church, I had the joy of seeing those two make a beautiful confession of faith and be received into the communicant membership of the church. For many such reasons I wonder whether or not absentee treatment of lost souls helps them or the pastor.

Organization has its place. So has corporate activity. But in as far as I have been able to judge from experience and observation, God promotes a man's spirituality more surely by leading him to engage in personal work than by letting him attend meetings that seem endless. Why devote half a day to learning what one can get from a book in half an hour? Such a time of mental repose will seem all the more welcome if a minister has been engaged in quiet talks with unsaved and unchurched neighbors and friends, one by one. Only at the risk of anemia in his own soul can any pastor delegate all of this work to others.

Pastoral Nurture

Ministerial growth likewise comes through pastoral nurture of boys and girls. The term here refers to the sort of quiet person-to-person ministry that Richard Baxter did at Kidderminster, and about which Horace Bushnell later wrote in *Christian Nurture* (1846). This book includes a chapter on "The Out-Populating Power of the Christian Stock." Bushnell meant that if the Church could keep and train for God all her own boys and girls there would be no limit to her growth and spiritual power. Both of those worthies believed in adult conversion, and so do I. Theologically I stand closer to Baxter than to Bushnell. With both of them I believe that it is far better to prevent juvenile delinquency than to deal with it after it bursts out and sweeps across the community like a forest fire.

Here I am stressing the fact that pastoral nurture of young boys and girls constitutes one of the pastor's main opportunities to do good for time and eternity. Also, this constant opportunity affords a way to keep growing like the One who in Galilee set a little child in the midst. Ideally this nurture may begin when the pastor confers with a man and a woman soon to be married. With them he may hold up the ideal of starting their married life together by kneeling to ask the blessing of God on their home and their wedded life. He may tell them the sweet idea of Augustine, that when our Lord speaks about two praying together he may refer to a bride and her husband. As for three, that may mean the two in their first prayer together after the birth of a baby. Why should not the first words that a baby hears on earth be those of prayer?

Among all the kind things that church friends have said about me, there is one that I cherish most. It refers to my work as pastor in a church that ministered largely to university folk. When I was leaving the field the chief executive of our denomination in that area said publicly, "I have been with Blackwood in all sorts of meetings for adults. I have repeatedly heard him lead in prayer. Never once have I failed to hear him tell the Heavenly Father about the heart needs of growing boys and girls." I still feel that such ministerial concern helps to make a man grow.

Here again a pastor ought not to delegate all his opportunity to become like the One who was never too busy with adults to show concern about children. Years ago at the historic Plymouth Church in Brooklyn the Sunday schools of the Empire State were holding their annual convention. In one of the main addresses the pastor, Henry Ward Beecher, said that he envied the teachers their opportunity to influence growing boys and girls. As a pulpiteer he coveted some such a privilege, but in Plymouth Church he said that he felt obliged to delegate all this work. The next speaker had come in late. He may not have heard this part of Beecher's brilliant address. At any rate this other man, unknown to us now, told the assembled throng:

"The Devil would never ask anything more of a minister than to have him feel that his mission was chiefly to the grown-up members of his congregation, while someone else was to look after the children." Then the speaker pointed to the entrance of Plymouth Church and declared: "I can see the Devil looking in at the door, and saying to the minister on this platform, 'Now you just stand here and fire away at the old folks, and I'll go around and steal the little ones—as the Indians steal ducks, swimming under them, catching them by the legs, and pulling them under.' "[1]

Pastoral nurture of the right sort begins with children but it includes the entire congregation. Such a movement also reaches out into the community. Both directly and through fellow workers the pastor ministers to persons of every age group, according to their spiritual needs. But the stress ought to fall largely on work in which many a church is failing dismally: spiritual nurture of little boys and girls. Much as we believe in adult evangelism we ought to make it unnecessary with our own little ones in home and church. What a privilege to lead them, one by one, into glad acceptance of the Lord Jesus as Saviour and Master, and then train them for valiant service in Kingdom and Church! In as far as a pastor excels in these beautiful ministries, his own soul keeps growing more Christlike.[2] Alas, the reverse may also hold true.

[1] See Edgar D. Jones, *The Royalty of the Pulpit* (New York: Harper & Bros., 1951), pp. 225-26.

[2] In general read a stimulating book, sometimes provocative, by Joseph E. McCabe, *The Power of God in a Parish Program* (Philadelphia: Westminster Press, 1958).

CHAPTER VII

Church Leadership

ONCE AGAIN WE ARE TO THINK ABOUT WORK FOR GOD AS A WAY to ministerial growth. In the local church and elsewhere the right sort of leadership by the pastor tends to develop in him every Christ-like virtue. Elsewhere I have dealt with the subject,[1] but from a different point of view. Here I stress the influence on the man who accepts the leadership of a congregation as a whole, with its various boards and organizations, as a part of the Holy Catholic Church. Mistakenly, a pastor may feel that in local church leadership he is doing secular work. He may regret that he cannot give himself exclusively to things spiritual (Acts 6:4). Here, as often elsewhere, it is hard to keep one's balance.

As everyone knows, the word pastor still means shepherd. Not only should he take loving care of every person in distress (Ps. 23). A local minister ought also to lead the flock as a whole, and that with skill (John 10; I Pet. 5:1-4, *et al.*) Indeed, he ought also to feel much concern about folds at a distance (John 10:16). This conception of pastoral oversight appears repeatedly in the Scriptures, and in church history. As an apt description of God's parish leader current writers have borrowed from Gregory the Great (d. 604) an expressive term, "the pastoral director." [2]

In the history of the Church almost every man who has excelled as a leader of God's people has kept growing spiritually. In Bible days think of Joseph, Moses, Nehemiah, and Paul.

[1] See my *Pastoral Leadership* (Nashville: Abingdon Press, 1949).

[2] See H. Richard Niebuhr, *The Purpose of the Church and Its Ministry* (New York: Harper & Brothers, 1956).

In times more nearly modern, among men not local pastors, think of John Wesley, William Booth, Dwight L. Moody, Hudson Taylor, and John R. Mott. Among men who excelled as pastors, consider Thomas Chalmers, Charles H. Spurgeon, John Watson (Ian Maclaren), Phillips Brooks, and George W. Truett. Why did every one of those worthies keep growing from decade to decade? Not least because he accepted God-given opportunities for leadership of a local church. Any reader can add still other examples from yesterday and today.

Growth Through Responsibility

"Responsibility teaches." These words stand at the head of a chapter in a current book, *For Future Doctors.*[3] On the basis of thirty-five years in the medical profession a leading official of the Rockefeller Foundation shows that the right sort of personal leadership develops the qualities of character that go to make up a first-class medical man. At a large hospital one of the leading professors broke his leg. Instead of looking outside for someone to take his place in the hospital, the professor turned over all his administrative duties to a young intern. In later years this former assistant testified that during those months of responsibility he had grown more than during any other part of his training.

In the parish ministry, also, responsibility teaches. At least it ought to do so. But the beneficial effects depend on many factors. For example, a young pastor should have a degree of fitness for the new tasks; he should accept them without grudging; and he should perform them with all his might. These principles apply to a pastor in his first charge, and in every later one. Even in a church comparatively small a young pastor accepts responsibility for an enterprise much more extensive, more varied, and more important than any department of a first-rate hospital.

[3] By Alan Gregg, M.D. (Chicago: University of Chicago Press, 1957).

Think of a young man a month after his graduation from seminary. Without any sort of "internship" he assumes the oversight of three hundred church members, with more than that many adherents. At least indirectly he becomes responsible for the church building and grounds; the paid staff, however limited; the leadership of various boards elected by the congregation; the activity of numerous societies, with their own selected officers; the church musicians and the ushers; and not a few connections with the community, and with the denomination. All of this sounds formidable.

Through these agencies the pastor is somehow responsible for the conduct of public worship, religious education, Christian nurture, pastoral care, inter-church relations, community betterment, nation-wide missions, and missions overseas. In most churches these days every such activity has various ramifications, and yet there is need of many things else, such as training the people to pray, and preparing the young folk for marriage in the Lord, and for parenthood. Looming above all of these objectives, some of the lay officers may look on the raising of money as the chief concern of the local church. In some cases they wish the pastor to raise it, and then let them spend it.

All of these relations and activities ought to be spiritual. For example, consider the raising of money to repair the windows of a church building fifty years old, or the erection of a native church in the French Cameroun. When Paul wrote his mighty Resurrection Chapter (I Cor. 15) he was holding up spiritual ideals. So was he in the succeeding verses (16:1-3) when he wrote about raising money for the relief of God's suffering poor. If a pastor today has the mind of Christ he may be as deeply spiritual when he guides in the raising of money for current expenses and benevolences as when he leads in prayer for missionaries in Pakistan. In all practical activities he ought to rely on spiritual means. He ought also to maintain his balance and his peace of mind. Otherwise he cannot keep on growing Christlike.

These practical qualities stand out in more than a few of the parables. According to a helpful book about the human aspects of our Lord's ministry, the parables show the type of character that He wishes to develop in His followers:

> Many of the Parables turn on energy. The trouble with men, He seems to say, is . . . sheer slackness; they will not put their minds to the thing before them, whether it be thought or action. Thus, for instance, the parable of the talents turns on energetic thought and decisive action. . . . On the other side, He is against the life of drift, the half-thought-out life."[4]

The parable of the talents has to do mainly with our making ready for the final return of our Lord. By implication this parable likewise sets forth principles of decisive action that ought to mark the leadership of a pastor today. In this parable the word talent means opportunity. Whenever the Lord's chosen leader makes the most of all his present opportunities, the reward may come in the form of an opportunity to lead in doing twice as much work. The reward also consists in commendation by the Master Workman. In other words, a minister who leads in doing the Lord's work in the Lord's way keeps growing in likeness to Him as the Ideal Worker.

What an ideal! How it differs from the facts in many a minister's life today! As for the difficulty in making and keeping pastoral leadership spiritual, or Christian, both in purpose and in method, I shall say nothing more just now. First we ought to think about the ideal, as it comes from our Lord. What then does it mean to look on executive and administrative work as holy unto the Lord? It means that work in view all comes from

[4] See T. R. Glover, *The Jesus of History* (New York: Grosset & Dunlap, 1917), pp. 130-31.

God; that the distribution of it among others depends largely on the pastor as chief; and that he does his full share of it with alacrity, as "a workman who has no need to be ashamed" (II Tim. 2:15*b*). Whatever a pastor does for the Lord gladly he learns to do well, and whatever he keeps on doing well he learns to do gladly.

Spirituality Through Work

Every such leader wishes the home church to become spiritual. A spiritual congregation (Eph. 5:25-27) means one where the stress falls on seeking the glory of God through promoting the welfare of people. The stress does not fall mainly on organization and machinery, or on equipment and money. The Lord knows that the home church has need of all these things as means to spiritual ends. He wishes the home church and its minister to seek first the Kingdom of God, which means doing the will of God. On this basis He promises to guide in securing all the things they need to do His holy will (Matt. 6:19-34, especially v. 33).

Hence the minister enjoys doing all he can to promote use of the Bible, not least in homes. He takes no rest until the church provides ways and means for every person, young or old, to know the Bible as the magna carta of Christianity. He likewise welcomes every opportunity to promote prayer in the homes of the people, and in larger circles throughout the congregation. He wishes everyone to engage in public worship as a matter of Christian habit, especially at the celebration of Baptism and the Lord's Supper. He gladly gives much thought to ways and means of winning the unsaved and the unchurched; to the moral betterment of the local community; and to the promotion of Missions, both in the homeland and beyond the seven seas.

A spiritual leader also pays constant attention to what Charles E. Jefferson calls "building the brotherhood." He looks on the home church, not as an organization with machinery like that of a country club, but as a family of God's redeemed children with simple ways of expressing their love for Him, for each other, and for others elsewhere. Jefferson makes a clear distinction between building a congregation and attracting a crowd. "An audience is a set of unrelated people drawn together by a short-lived attraction. . . . An audience is a crowd, a church is a family. An audience is a gathering, a church is a fellowship. An audience is a collection, a church is an organism. An audience is a heap of stones, a church is a temple." [5]

Such a church family keeps active in spiritual work. In various groups and in all sorts of ways the people are "diligent in business, fervent in spirit, serving the Lord." Under the guidance and restraint of the Holy Spirit, and the leadership of the pastor, they seek the goals that have passed before us, and any others that local and temporary circumstances may require. For example, if changing needs call for a new sanctuary, or the enlargement of the present one, they gladly accept the opportunity to glorify their God this way. All the while they give more gladly and more largely for the promotion of these activities at home and elsewhere. Many of them think in terms of the tithe as the minimum, with frequent additional thank offerings. Indeed, certain congregations among Seventh-day Adventists think of the norm as 25 per cent.

With any such congregational ideals the Lord is well pleased. So is He with the pastor who gladly devotes himself to the promotion of all this spiritual life and work. The minister knows that in large measure the growth of congregational life depends on abundance of work by laymen. But he never becomes so busy with other things as to stint the time he should devote to making ready for the pulpit and to engaging in pastoral care. Indeed, he uses these services to promote every spiritual cause

[5] See *Building the Church* (New York: The Macmillan Company, 1910), p. 67.

dear to his heart. As for practical ways and means of translating lofty ideals into feasible programs, he trusts the Lord to use the local friends with whom he shares visions of a spiritual church, a friendly church, an active church, and a generous church—all for the glory of God through His blessing on "the diligent use of the outward and ordinary means of grace."

Here let the stress fall on these activities as God-given ways of developing a minister's powers through the exercise of all his spiritual muscles. While self-development is never his motive, that should always be a result, a by-product of what most blesses the people. Whenever he leads them to grow in grace through the joyous use of God-given resources, the pastor himself shares bountifully in the waters that overflow from these wellsprings of God.

Blessing Through Drudgery

The chapters so far have made clear that the Lord expects a pastor to work hard, always for spiritual ends. No man fit for the cloth wishes to avoid strenuous toil. But many of us keep lamenting that we can not give ourselves exclusively to "spiritual work." Amen, but provided the term means doing whatever the Lord wishes a man to do in building up the brotherhood that we know as the home church. To make this point of view clear, without seeming to be unkind, let me review my own early experiences in the pastorate, where I had three years of self-directed apprenticeship and fourteen years of increasing ministerial joy.

"As a pastoral director" I enjoyed all my work in the pulpit and in other sorts of pastoral teaching; my duties as a shepherd of souls and a counselor; my share in the general oversight of the congregation and all its organized activities; and my part in what we call the larger work of the Kingdom. But I begrudged the time I had to spend on executive details, not least in keeping records. Only gradually did I discover that any self-respecting physician, printer, or public school teacher has fully as many petty details, and has learned to "take them in his stride."

Later when I became a full-time professor I plunged at once into work that consisted largely of details. From that time to this I have had no assistant minister, no secretary, no board of officers glad to help, and no host of other lay friends eager to show love for God by relieving me of what I used to call my burdens. I have come to believe that when a man accepts details as an integral part of the day's work, and deals with them as well as he can, he should discover that what he once regarded as his cross has become to him a means of blessing.

Every day for years I have thanked God for giving me work to do, and strength to do it. Gradually I have learned that work involving many details may be God's chosen way of teaching me what I could not learn if through life I took an elective course and left for other hands all the time-consuming details. This point of view appears in an old-time essay by William C. Gannett. In writing on "Blessed Be Drudgery" he was not thinking about the work of a parish minister. Still the shoe seems to fit the clerical foot:

> We have to go, morning by morning, through rain and through shine, through headache and heartache, to the appointed spot and to the given task. We have to stick to that work through eight or ten hours, long after rest would be sweet. We must keep in good temper with children, with neighbors, and with others, not seven times, but seventy times seven. We must watch that besetting sin today and tomorrow and every day.
>
> In short, without much matter where our work may lie, it is because of the rut and the plod, the grind and the humdrum, that we at last get laid the foundations of character: attention and promptness, accuracy and firmness, patience and self-denial, and all the rest.
>
> Then beyond all books, all class-work, all special opportunities of what I call my education, it is the drill and the pressure of my

daily task that is my schoolmaster. Yet, fool that I am, this pressure of my daily task is what I growl at as my drudgery!

Blessed be drudgery! [6]

Blessedness Through Sharing

In order to keep the record straight, let us carry the ideal one stage farther. As every reader knows, a wise "pastoral director" does nothing that he should get others to do (Exod. 18:13-26; Acts 6:1-7). Then he has time and serenity for all that God wishes him to do. In pursuance of this ideal more than a few of our larger congregations have employed expert laymen as "Church Business Administrators." At a recent annual convention meeting in Los Angeles these men singled out as examples of "good financial health" the Hollywood [United] Presbyterian Church, the First Congregational Church of Los Angeles, and Seventh-day Adventist churches in general.

At Hollywood the First [United] Presbyterian Church is the largest in the denomination. Currently it reports 7,228 communicant members, with 5,929 persons enrolled in the Bible School. The senior minister, Raymond Irving Lindquist, assures me that in the study he now has much more time and freedom from care than when he served as pastor of a congregation and Bible School not a third as large. In that other field many of us watched him grow through glad acceptance of responsibility as a "pastoral director." Now we know that he still has enough responsibility to keep his spiritual muscles from becoming flabby through misuse.

What has all this to do with the fairly young pastor of what we call an "average church"? To this question we shall return later, and more than once. For the present let us agree that whether a congregation be small, large, or of medium size, it looks to the "pastoral director" for leadership. God seems to have meant it to be so. Let us also agree, perhaps at first hesi-

[6] Used by permission of Review and Herald Publications Associations, Tacoma Park, Washington, D.C.

tantly, that work for God in promoting a needed building program ought to seem as spiritual as that of preparing sermons. The difference is that in one case a wise leader delegates almost everything; in the other he does the spade work himself. Let us agree, too, that doing any work by God's appointment ought to become a means of grace to the pastor. So let the local leader of the Kingdom enterprise thank God for every opportunity to do good, and by doing good, to grow better.

CHAPTER VIII

Bodily Discipline

THE SPIRITUAL GROWTH OF A MINISTER DEPENDS LARGELY ON what he does with his body. The length of his active ministry and its usefulness from day to day may be affected by habits of which he is not aware. All of this has to do with psychosomatic medicine. Popularly this terms relates to the influence of mind on body, and of body on mind. Ideally, they both work together in harmony while doing the will of God. Actually, one often interferes with the other. "What therefore God has joined together, let not man put asunder" (Matt. 19:6). Here we need not think of any extreme case that would call for drastic surgery of body or soul. Let us rather consider the hypothetical person, "an average minister." What about his body?

The Holiness of the Body

The Bible teaches every believer to look on his body as belonging to God. Among all the wonders of His creation, nothing visible seems to compare in importance with the human body. By creation, by preservation, and by redeeming grace the Lord has shown how highly He regards the body of His child. Everywhere the Bible teaches that the body of a believer ought to be holy. This means to be like God, in the sense that He is far removed from everything unworthy and unclean. This idea of holiness for the body as well as the soul stands out supremely in Baptism and in the Lord's Supper. In Baptism the water symbolizes cleansing of both soul and body. In the Lord's Supper everything centers around the words of the Redeemer: "This is my body, which is broken for you."

Above all other men, a pastor ought to keep his body holy

unto the Lord. This truth stands out in Leviticus, a manual for priests. With all the changes that have come to us in Christian ways of worship, those early rites among a childlike people still have a symbolic meaning. In the "ordination" of a young priest (Lev. 8-9) nearly all the appointed actions had to do with his body. In addition to animal sacrifices that symbolized forgiveness of his sins, and the dedication of himself to God, think about the washing of his body, the putting on of distinctive apparel, and the wearing of a breastplate with the names of the twelve tribes, whom he was to represent before God.

To a childlike people those rites symbolized that God wished His local representative to be holy and to be useful. The element of usefulness appeared in the anointing with oil, which means to us enduement with the Holy Spirit, as the source of holiness and ability to serve. When applied to the right ear, the right thumb, and the right toe, the anointing oil showed that henceforth the young man was to serve the people of God with his entire body. In the presence of human need, he was to hear the cry or the whisper of anyone in distress, to use his hand in helping anyone who had fallen down, and his foot in walking where he could do most good for others.

In Old Testament times these ideals were often "more honored in the breach than the observance." Still the ideals stood out in Holy Writ, and there they stand today. In the New Testament dispensation the forms have changed almost completely. Still the ideals hold in forms more lofty. Throughout the New Testament the body occupies a much larger place than we usually suppose. Whenever the epistles mention the body, as they often do, present-day commentators and preachers usually interpret the words "spiritually." They leave the impression that spirituality has little to do with a man's body. But why "spiritualize" plain Christian ethics?

For example, take the beginning of what we used to call "The Christian Endeavor Chapter" (Rom. 12). The opening sentence calls on believers to "present their bodies a living sacrifice." As a boy I used to attend Christian Endeavor regularly. Throughout manhood I have heard and read many sermons and addresses about this and kindred passages of Holy Writ. Never once, except from my own lips, have I ever heard a sermon or a prayer that voiced strong concern about the welfare of a young man's body. To judge from many sermons and books, one might conclude that the hearers and readers were disembodied spirits. Perhaps my experience has been exceptional. If it seems to be so, read the commentaries about this passage, and then search for Biblical sermons about the will of the Lord for the body of a young believer.

On the contrary, in England a theologian has written an able little book about *The Body: A Study in Biblical Theology*.[1] If this book receives the attention it deserves it will do much to correct the mistaken impressions of pastors who have tried to dedicate their souls to God, and have never thought of doing the same with their bodies. Herein has lain one of the chief weaknesses in the home training and the higher education of young clergymen. Now listen to the British divine. Here follows the central core of his book, which calls for a study of New Testament sources, in the spirit of prayer, which may include contrition:

"Without exaggeration the concept of the body forms the keystone of Paul's theology. . . . Here, with the exception of the doctrine of God, are represented all the main tenets of the Christian faith." In all fairness we ought to remember that the apostle Paul often spoke of the body in a sense largely figurative. We ought also to recognize that in some cases when he wrote about the body he referred to flesh and blood. If he had not, how could he have dealt properly with the sins of men in Corinth, which seems to have been a cesspool of physical sin?

"Do you not know that your body is a temple of the Holy Spirit within you, which you have from God? You are not your

[1] By John A. T. Robertson (London: S. C. M. Press, 1953), p. 9 *passim*.

own; you were bought with a price. So glorify God in your body." (I Cor. 6:19-20 R.S.V.) In view of what precedes and what follows these searching words, no minister dares to ignore the reference to a believer as God's appointed custodian of his body. On the Continent certain learned theologians have become so much concerned about Christian doctrine that even in writing about 1 Corinthians one of them ignores its ethics and considers it solely as doctrine divorced from moral application. Is it any wonder that William James once wrote about "a certain blindness in human beings"?

The Dedication of the Body

At his ordination, if not before, what should a young minister do with his body? Let him dedicate it all to God. Every man ought to do so, repeatedly, but no one so completely as a pastor. As with the building where he will serve as minister, this body needs to be set apart for its holy uses. The consecration can come only from God. In the original form "to dedicate" meant to give completely to God; "to consecrate" meant His making holy what one had dedicated to Him. In the plural these ideas appear in the opening verse of the twelfth chapter of Romans: "I appeal to you therefore, brethren, by the mercies of God, to present your bodies as a living sacrifice" (Rom. 12:1*a* R.S.V.). Here the stress falls, not on a single act of dedication for life, but on daily acts of oblation, like the Hebrew burnt-offerings, which were completely consumed.

About all these ethical matters today, laymen feel increasingly uncertain. From the pastor they have a right to expect a personal demonstration of what Paul teaches about bodily discipline. In a city famous for its stadium and Corinthian Games he held up an ideal in terms of athletics: "Every athlete exercises self-control in all things. . . . I do not run aimlessly, I do not box as one beating the air; but I pommel my body and subdue it, lest after preaching to others I should be disqualified" (I Cor. 9:25-27 R.S.V.). Occasionally one reads about a minister who has been silenced and unfrocked because of flagrant bodily sins. If every pastor who in less sensational ways neglects this earthly temple were subject to church discipline, how many of us would go free?

In his Yale Lectures Phillips Brooks told future ministers that their work would "involve the whole man, and [that] the whole man is both soul and body together. Therefore the Lord brings the perfectly healthy body with the perfectly sound soul." Without trying to explain the facts, either physically or otherwise, think of the following ministers whose popular appeal has been due in no small measure to mastery of bodily powers: Brooks himself, Henry Ward Beecher, Joseph Parker, and "Billy" Graham. In the ministry, it seems, things that matter most lie at the mercy of things that seem not to matter much.

Not every pastor has a commanding physique or perfect health. Neither does every congregation worship in a temple without earthly flaws. But the custodian of temple or body should do his utmost to keep it clean and to make it useful. Like Paul with his "stake in the flesh," or George Matheson with the onset of his blindness, a pastor may have physical handicaps beyond his control. If so, why despair? It would not be difficult to show that either Paul or Matheson became a more useful and a more Christlike person after he "made friends with his infirmity." But still the ideal for a minister today ought to be that of a healthy soul in a healthy body.

This truth came to me years ago from E. Stanley Jones. He told me that in his earlier ministry he had not learned how to deal effectively with his body. As a consequence he seems to have suffered from the sort of physical ups and downs that come to many a man who unintentionally neglects and abuses his body. At a certain stage of middle life Jones took himself in hand, dedicated to God all his bodily resources, and determined that he would do everything in his power to keep that body well and strong. Without knowing anything about the subsequent facts in the case, I have from a distance watched him do far more work during the latter half of his ministry than during the former part. "Even down to old age," he has kept on working hard. Today I thank God for what E. Stanley Jones taught me about the conservation of all a man's bodily resources.

The Care of a Man's Body

What Paul says about the temple may apply in part to a man's automobile. What a minister gets out of his car depends largely on whether or not he treats it well. Once every six months, in our city, a person has to take his automobile to an impartial expert for inspection, and have it approved from the front bumper to the tail light. If anything vital is missing, that part must be replaced. If anything is out of order, it must be repaired. Is it unreasonable to ask that a minister take equally good care of his body? Once a year, preferably twice, he may go to an expert in internal medicine and have a complete check-up. After that he can live according to the direction of an expert whose business it is to keep a person well and strong.

At the College of Physicians and Surgeons in New York City a certain graduation class numbered 175. Forty years later, when those men should have been at their prime, 60 had died, seven of them in the past year. At the annual reunion a distinguished member asked, "How many of you have had a complete physical checkup in the past twelve months?" Not a single hand went up, not even his own. Then he moved that the class choose from its number a committee, whose business it would be to keep its members alive. The motion prevailed, the committee was chosen, and it went to work. Those experts found that the gall bladder man had a gall bladder infection, the hernia man needed an operation for hernia. But the check-up did not all bring bad news. The heart man did not have heart disease, as he had supposed. Because of those expert findings, and the resulting discipline, the death rate among those men began to drop. For a time it almost disappeared.[2]

Experts in internal medicine report that many a breakdown in middle life comes from overeating, overweight, and overindulgence in physical pleasures not wrong unless carried to excess. With an exception here and there, clergymen keep free from drunkenness, gambling, and adultery, the spectacular besetting sins. But they do not show equal concern about "weights" that keep a pastor from excelling as a spiritual athlete. In Hebrews 12:1 the "weight" to be laid aside does not refer to anything wrong in itself. As for its identity, each man has to find that out for himself, partly under the care of a medical expert.

In the case of a certain professor of theology the experts found that his gall bladder had begun to disintegrate, and that it had to be removed. Afterward the professor said to the surgeon, the foremost man in his field, "Do you know what caused my gall bladder trouble?"

"Yes, it was overeating."

"Do you know when the trouble began?"

"Yes, I do, to a day."

"Tell me."

"When you began to overeat."

If experts had not interfered, that professor would have died in a few months. Then the officiating clergymen might have declared: "Blessed are the dead which die in the Lord." Since when has the Lord been responsible for a pastor's overeating, and for twenty years of wasted life? In the light of sayings in Job and in the Epistles (II Cor. 12:7) the physical ills of a good man may come from the devil, not from God.

As with everything else in Christian discipline, concern about one's body may go too far, and in the wrong direction. Whatever the regimen, it calls for common sense, with concern for

[2] See Martin Gumpert, M.D., *You Are Younger than You Think* (New York: Duell, Sloan, and Pearce, 1944), pp. 3-5.

the comfort of others. According to a recent biography, Philip Melanchthon seems to have carried self-imposed asceticism too far. In his diet, and no doubt in other things physical, he was most abstemious. He looked so "emaciated, exhausted, nervous, and anxious," that Luther bade him care for his body and cease killing himself by imaginary obedience to God. The robust Reformer declared that while Melanchthon was preparing his revision of the *Augsburg Confession* (1531) he worried over every preposition, noun, and verb. So Luther warned his scholarly colleague: "We serve God also by taking rest and holiday." [8]

A ministerial friend suggests that a person can look at his body in one of three ways. First, that of our Lord, in His expression of love for others, in whose place He was soon to die: "This is my body, which is broken for you." By the giving of that blessed body He brought about our redemption, a completed work that we cannot comprehend, and in which we can never take an active part. But from the Cross with its self-giving love every one of us can learn the Christian attitude toward his body: "My body for others! Whether I eat, or drink, or whatever I do, let it be for the glory of God and the welfare of others."

On the other hand, a worldly man has a practical philosophy far different: "My body for myself!" What I do with my body in the way of eating, drinking, and other bodily indulgences concerns nobody but me. I am the captain of my body." As for the out-and-out wicked man, he says, or at least he thinks: "Thy body for me." What that means in terms of slavery, prostitution, child labor, tenement housing, and other forms of social evil does not directly concern us now, except in contrast with the Christian ideal.

Any minister of Christ Jesus today ought to accept His claim to be the Lord of a man's body. Now and again the pastor will set this truth forth as it appears in the Bible. "I am eager to sat-

[8] See Clyde Manschreck, *Melanchthon the Quiet Reformer* (Nashville: Abingdon Press, 1958), pp. 183, 308.

isfy him [the Lord Jesus], whether in the body or away from it; for we have all to appear without disguise before the tribunal of Christ, each to be requited for what he has done with his body, well or ill." (II Cor. 5:9-10, Moffatt.)

The Discipline of Life

This idea of bodily discipline leads out into a broader field at which we can only glance. In the Providence of God ministerial development comes most surely through triumph over difficulties that may seem insuperable. Among the stalwarts in the Hebrew "Hall of Fame" (Heb. 11) almost every one grew strong in faith through surmounting difficulties. In the New Testament almost every worthy became like his Lord through acceptance of exacting discipline as an essential factor of a good man's life. In a world where the Son of God had to die because of sin, anyone who wishes to become like Him needs to follow in His pathway of "peril, toil, and pain."

This idea of discipline for Christ's sake stands out everywhere in the life of Paul and in his Epistles. In writing to young Titus, the apostle uttered a truth that must have startled the young minister. Titus may have written to the veteran missioner about the difficulties of pastoral work in Crete. Paul's reply confirmed the young man's judgment about the difficulties in that field. Then the apostle said: "For this cause left I thee in Crete" (Tit. 1:5). Why? Partly because Paul knew that a young pastor could become strong and good through acceptance of a hard field, and through triumph over its difficulties.

Under God, the value of such discipline depends largely on the spirit with which a man accepts his lot, and on the faith with which he surmounts its difficulties. In view of the stony heights that he must climb, a Christian pilgrim's heart can sing: "There let the way appear steps unto heaven." Because he knows that stony ways are "in mercy given" he can face life's obstacles with "apostolic optimism" (Rom. 8:28). For such reasons Browning would have God's pilgrim sing ("Rabbi Ben Ezra"):

> Then, welcome each rebuff
> That turns earth's smoothness rough,
> Each sting that bids not sit nor stand but go!
> Be our joy three-parts pain!
> Strive, and hold cheap the strain;
> Learn, nor account the pang; dare, never
> grudge the throe.

CHAPTER IX

Personal Contacts

WE HAVE BEEN THINKING ABOUT VARIOUS WAYS IN WHICH A MINister can grow in likeness to the Master. Under God, everything so far seems to depend on him and his conscious efforts. There is, however, another side of the matter, probably a more important one. While nobody can measure with a yardstick the stages in the growth of a man's soul, or account for the increase of his spiritual stature, it may well be that his development as a Christlike person depends on other persons much more than on himself. Through the silent influence of other people who love him, a pastor ought to keep growing more like God.

Contacts with Many Persons

"I am a part of all that I have met." So sings Tennyson in "Ulysses." "No man is an iland, intire of itself." So says whimsical John Donne (d. 1631) in words that a modern novel has made famous. "Any man's death diminishes me, because I am involved in mankinde; and therefore never send to know for whom the bell tolls; it tolls for thee." [1] Let us agree that any young minister is largely what others have made him, especially those who have loved him in the Lord. As a rule such an influence comes to him unconsciously.

This truth shines out in a well-known sermon by Horace Bushnell, "Unconscious Influence" (John 20:8). He says what every active clergyman should take to heart: many persons busily engaged in religious work attain little in the way of spiritual growth, whereas others not so conspicuous for "busyness" keep

[1] See *The Devotions,* No. XVIII; also, *For Whom the Bell Tolls,* by Ernest Hemingway, 1940, not a lily-white tale.

on growing. Throughout the sermon the Hartford divine keeps insisting that a person becomes good by having his soul quietly exposed to the influence of light and love, especially love, both human and divine. With special reference to himself as a minister of The Methodist Church this idea appears in a book by D. T. Niles, a brilliant native son of Ceylon:

> I am a sinner for whom Jesus died. . . . We must learn to live by this love with which we are loved. Only so do we learn to live at all. . . . In my home I do not live as a person under obligation to love my wife and children. I live as a person who is loved by them. . . . The love of God and of man become a possibility only to those who know what it is to be loved.[2]

At the time of his graduation from college a future minister owes practically everything, under God, to those who have loved him. At home, at church, at school, and everywhere else, he may thus far owe more to women than to men. Before many years, after he has become a husband and father, he may appreciate what John Ruskin says in *Sesame and Lilies:* "No man ever lived a right life who has not been chastened by a woman's love, strengthened by her courage, and guided by her discretion. . . . The soul's armor is never well set to the heart unless a woman's hand has braced it, and it is only when she has braced it too loosely that the honor of manhood fails."

From now onward we may be thinking more about the help that comes from good men, but we ought to remember these words from Ruskin. In *The Little Minister,* by Sir James M. Barrie, a young pastor owes everything to his mother. All these estimates of the "human situation" point to a truth that now serves as a kind of thesis: among the many good men at work in any community, a pastor has the best opportunity to grow like his Lord. More largely than anyone else who longs to be

[2] See *Preaching the Gospel of the Resurrection* (Philadelphia: Westminster Press, 1954), p. 45.

good, a parish minister lives and moves and has his being among people who stand ready to love him, and thus become agents of God in his transformation.

Contacts in the First Charge

In his first charge a minister finds himself at once among people who wish to know him well and love him much. They take him into their hearts and their homes. Soon they begin to share with him their joys, as well as their sorrows. In *The Little Minister* the mother says to her son: "It's hardly fair that your hands should be so full of other people's troubles." The young man replies: "They fill only one hand, mother. I carry the people's joys in the other hand, and that keeps me erect. The joys have outweighed the sorrows."

Such a pastor soon falls in love with the home church. He begins to love the building. He learns much from the elderly custodian, who may serve only part time. In my own ministry everyone who successfully acted in this capacity taught and showed me much that I needed to know. At a time when I was tempted to feel discontented with my lot, and to reach out after bigger things, a caretaker explained to me his practical philosophy. His brother served well as one of the elders, and the custodian felt grateful for that honor to their family. But he told me that he felt as much called and honored of God as if he too served as a spiritual leader of the congregation. What a privilege and a joy to be such "a door-keeper in the house of the Lord"! In that case the less conspicuous brother helped the pastor more than the other man could.

By mingling with the lay officers of a church a young minister can learn all sorts of spiritual lessons that he has not been taught in school or in books. While still young in the work I wrote for a church paper an article on "What the Elders Have Taught Me." Now that I look back on seventeen years in the pastorate I regard the influence of lay officers as among the most formative elements in all my life. When occasionally I hear something unkind about a domineering deacon or a listless lay leader, I cudgel by brains in vain to find any such recollections. I learned to love those men, not least because they first loved me, for Jesus' sake. By example rather than precept they showed me what I needed to know. Most of all they impressed me by "sweet reasonableness."

Much the same principle applies to the superintendent of the church school, the treasurer of the church, the ushers, the friends in the choir, and all the other unpaid leaders of congregational life and work. Down in his heart a pastor knows that almost every one of them, while not perfect, has been an agent of God's blessing. For many such reasons an Episcopal rector, afterwards an honored bishop, advised me as a younger clergyman: "Never begrudge the time and effort it takes to confer with a lay worker, or with a committee that works deliberately. If you enter into the spirit of any such conference, you will learn what you could not get in any other way." To all this I now say a hearty Amen.

Contact with a Pastor's Pastor

Thus we have been thinking about bright aspects of a parish ministry. Ideally, every person one meets ought to be an agent of God's helpfulness. Later we shall think more about the darker side of such things. Simply because a minister has to live and work with people not yet perfect, he often feels the need of a pastor in whom the younger man can confide. Somewhere in the community, or not far away, he can find a "father confessor" to whom the distraught young minister can pour out his troubles. The older friend may not know what the younger one should do, but the act of confiding in a sympathetic soul has a way of bringing guidance or restraint from the Lord.

"The act of confiding in human sympathy, the consciousness that a fellow-being is listening with patient pity, prepares the soul for that stronger leap by which faith grasps the idea of the divine sympathy." [3] So writes George Eliot in a work of fiction that every pastor ought often to read. She is speaking about an inconspicuous minister, a two-talent man, and the way he brings the peace of God to the heart of a gifted woman who has become a bond slave to strong drink.

Often help from a pastor comes indirectly. In Boston an earnest young man once faced a difficult problem that he could not begin to solve. One evening by appointment he went to confer with Phillips Brooks. After a while in that man's genial presence the young fellow came away, knowing that he had found an honorable way out of his dilemma. Then he remembere that he had not mentioned the matter to Brooks. In later years this younger man, George Herbert Palmer, became the Harvard University professor of ethics, a subject that he made to live, because he loved it as he would love a daughter.[4] One day in class he told about his early experience of being guided into the path of duty simply by sitting for a while in the company of a pastor who knew the Lord, and who cared for a young man with a troubled heart.

At times even an experienced pastor may need to consult a wise, understanding friend. Whatever the nature or the cause of a minister's perplexity, he can always find within reach a mature Christian ready to listen and extend both sympathy and help. After a visitor has sought and found such counsel, he will come away a humbler and a better man. In the new light that he gets on an old problem he may learn how to deal with much the same issue the next time it emerges in his own counsel room. As in the medical world, a wise physician of the soul soon sees the folly of trying singlehanded to solve every problem, and treat every case. On the other hand, many an older minister

[3] See "Janet's Repentance," in *Scenes of Clerical Life,* 1858 (Boston: Thos. Y. Crowell & Co., n.d.), p. 325.

[4] See his charming biography of his wife, *The Life of Alice Freeman Palmer* (Boston: Houghton Mifflin Company, 1908).

has thanked God for the privilege of serving unofficially as a "pastor pastorum."

Contacts with Various Churchmen

Even when no cloud darkens a man's sky, he can gain much help through loving fellowship with other clergymen. While young he may well seek out older men, whereas an older man often gains more through mingling with young ministers. Many choice spirits belong to various branches of the Christian church. Without being at all sectarian Phillips Brooks used to say that different branches of Christendom resembled beds of flowers in an old-time garden. To the beauty and fragrance of the garden as a whole each bed made a contribution all its own. For this reason any minister can learn much of lasting worth from brethren in any evangelical church.

In the older denominations we sometimes forget that many of the Lord's choicest spirits do not belong to "standard-brand" churches. In my own early years our people on both sides of the house kept themselves aloof from believers who dotted their i's and crossed their t's in a different way. In recent years I have gained much from fellowship with brethren in various bodies sometimes called "newer churches." I do not now refer to Christian Scientists, Jehovah's Witnesses, and followers of Father Divine. But I thank God for spiritual helpfulness and uplift from various groups who accept the Christ of the Bible and His Cross; for example, the Christian and Missionary Alliance, the Church of God, the Church of the Nazarene, groups of Mennonites, and not least, the Seventh-day Adventists.

If I have gained nothing else from these loving contacts, I have at least had an opportunity to grow humble, and to broaden my religious horizon. In every experience of fellowship with such friends I have found that they excel in respects where I have been weak. Often I have learned from them how to express Christian emotion without losing self-control. I have also seen a living commentary on the "testimony psalms," about thirty in all. As one of them sings, "Let the redeemed of the Lord say so." (Ps. 107:2*a*). Say what? That they are redeemed! In the spirit of such uplifting fellowship with people whose beliefs differ in detail from my own, I love to sing with Frederick W. Faber:

> For the love of God is broader than the measure of man's mind,
> And the heart of the Eternal is most wonderfully kind.

Now that we have come to the end of the first part of this book let us glance back. We have looked at various means and agents that God employs in enabling a pastor to keep growing through the years: Scripture reading, intercessory prayer, intellectual labor, pastoral activity, congregational leadership, bodily discipline, and personal contacts. In view of all these ideals and opportunities, every experienced pastor ought to ask himself: "Why have I not become more like my Lord? Surely I have had all sorts of incentives and opportunities to keep growing. Wherein have I fallen short?" By way of seeking answers, let us now turn to familiar obstacles that stand in the way of a pastor's spiritual growth. Fortunately, not all these obstacles appear in the pathway of any one minister. If they did, a pastor might find it hard to say:

> The lines are fallen unto me in pleasant places;
> Yea, I have a goodly heritage. (Ps. 16:6.)

PART TWO

Obstacles to Growth

CHAPTER X

Ministerial Sins

LIKE EVERY OTHER CALLING, THE MINISTRY HAS ITS TEMPTATIONS and sins. When a man becomes a minister he does not cease to be a man. Like his Lord he may be spiritually tempted more than other men. The devil still loves a shining mark. When he sees a man striving to be good and grow better, the devil longs to drag him down. Hence one ought often to think, and occasionally to preach, about the temptations of a person who stands out on the Lord's side. First one should ask Him to turn the searchlight on one's own soul, and help one to see what evil lurks there (Ps. 139:1, 24).

One could write an entire book [1] about the obstacles to a pastor's growth. Even to list most of them would take much time. A Lutheran professor singles out three: a tendency to shine, to whine, and to recline. Here we shall look for the sources of such disorders. Practically all of them flow from the seven deadly sins. So we shall follow the classic list, which seems to have come from Gregory the Great (d. 604). For convenience we shall follow a different order. First we shall look at the three that many of us find most detrimental to spiritual growth. Then we shall look at four others that may keep a good man from growing better. Fortunately no one of us has to combat all seven at the same time.

Ministerial Sins That Seem Common

"Deadly sins" means "capital" ones inimical to spiritual progress. By common consent the first place goes to pride.

[1] See Ralph G. Turnbull, *A Minister's Obstacles* (Westwood, N.J.: Fleming H. Revell Co., 1946).

According to John Baillie of Edinburgh, and other theologians today, pride is the characteristic sin of the modern man. Many a person prides himself on not committing murder and adultery, and engaging in gambling. He forgets that our Lord looks on pride as more deadly than all of these. Pride here is trying to put self in the place of sovereignty that belongs to God. Such a spirit seems foreign to the essence of Christianity, which stresses humility as a prime requisite for holiness. Surely a minister of God ought to be humble in His presence, and modest in dealing with men (Matt. 5:3, 5). Even so, among the most conscientious clergymen today pride still remains Soul Enemy Number One. From pride flow nearly all other ministerial sins, whether or not they seem deadly.

Pride. In the ministry at first everything conspires to make a young man proud. In the home church as a candidate for the holy office he is singled out as a hero. In college he belongs to a select group who meet to share visions of coming distinction. In the seminary everything practical centers around him as the key leader in promoting the Kingdom by building up the local church. In his student charge dear old ladies praise every sermon as a masterpiece. In his first pastorate he immediately becomes "the observed of all observers." Soon the local house of God may become known as "Mr. Hunter's church." In the pulpit during the sermon he alone may stand under a spotlight. Elsewhere he may unconsciously resemble a distinguished divine who was said to "strut while sitting down."

Not every pastor goes so far toward the adoration of self. But many of us have been headed in that direction. By way of a quick and easy proof, let any reader make a list of able ministers whom he knows to excel in humility.

Then let him ask a group of honest friends if he can qualify. In my own experience I can recall one and another, here and there. In each case the man stood out among his brethren as an exception to the general rule. Worst of all, down in my heart I know that I am one of the worst offenders. For this reason I have seldom dared to preach or write about humility and pride. Often I test myself by the saying of James Denney: "No man can bear witness to Christ and himself at the same time" (*Studies in Theology,* p. 161). This applies to preaching and to everything else that a man does for God. He does his best work only when he calls no special attention to himself, "Therefore let any one who thinks that he stands take heed lest he fall" (I Cor. 10:12).

A minister's pride puts him out of right relations with God. Like the Pharisee in the parable, even when a pastor prays his pride may keep his petitions from ascending above his head. If pride grows, as it tends to do, his Godlikeness goes down. Pride also interferes with a man's effectiveness as a pastor and counselor, and as a church leader. He resents constructive criticism, and spurns advice. Only last week I had a long distance call from another state inquiring about a certain minister. The officers in a large church wished to learn about the local reputation of a gifted clergyman. "With a single exception he has everything we want, but we wonder if he is as cocky as he seems." I assured them that he was not. But I knew why that particular church wanted a pastor who was not unlike his Lord.

Worst of all, from the present angle, pride interferes with the growth of a man's soul. Even though a minister daily goes through all the customary acts of devotion, the spiritual value depends on the climate of his soul. Pride dwarfs or destroys all sorts of incipient goodness. As for the remedy, it may have to come from "the Celestial Surgeon." The soul cure may begin at the foot of the Cross. In full view of Him who "humbled himself and became obedient unto death," a man finds pardon, cleansing, and peace, which come through contrition and confession, it may be as by fire. Then a man learns how to put God first, others second, and self last. All of this rings out in the noblest of our hymns:

When I survey the wondrous Cross
  On which the Prince of Glory died,
My richest gain I count but loss,
  And pour contempt on all my pride.

Envy. Pride leads to envy. It was so at the Cross. Among "the sins that crucified Jesus," one of the worst was envy, and that on the part of "pious" churchmen, cursed with pride (Mark 15:10) ! So with many an able minister today envy stands out as Soul Enemy Number Two. When a pastor thinks more highly of himself than of God, or of anyone else, he resents seeing others outstrip him in what worldly men term a "rat race" for preferment. No wonder William Law spoke of envy as "the most ungenerous, base, and wicked passion that can enter the heart of man"!

If any reader feels that he is exempt, let him ask a few simple questions: "When the appointments were read out in the last Conference, how did I feel? What did I say? Did I thank God that this man or that had received a promotion he richly deserved? Did I make it a point sincerely to tell him so? Or did I sneak off to the cloak room and join in the ministerial chorus of complaints?" In matters of the sort the pastors of no one denomination have any monopoly. Of course everyone knows that churches and bishops may make mistakes about placing ministers. But even the Almighty could not grant all the desires of clergymen whose hearts are full of pride and envy. They magnify their own abilities, and are blind to the powers of other men whom God blesses.

On the other hand, in our denomination a certain divine became known as never having said anything but good about a brother minister. This Greatheart repeatedly went out of his way to tell an obscure pastor something true, kind, and encouraging. Before this older man went home to God I met him twice, and that only in passing. Each time he told me something that I shall remember with thanksgiving as long as I live. Why did I as an unknown pastor lay up in memory two sentences from a passing stranger whom the Lord had honored? Surely because such a man seems rare, even in the ministry. This one had in his heart the Christlike love that casts out pride and envy. In the words of the Apostle, a Christlike minister "thinketh no evil [about his brethren]; rejoiceth not in iniquity, but rejoiceth in the truth" (I Cor. 13:5*d*-6).

Covetousness. Covetousness and envy often seem to be twin sisters. Indeed it is difficult to distinguish between the two children of pride. Often a pastor envies men other than ministers, but more often he covets laymen's property. For convenience we can think of the two vices as separate. Envy relates chiefly to the other person and his gifts, or attainments; covetousness has to do with his possessions. With a layman as neighbor the pastor may covet his house, his car, or his bank account. With a brother minister, his parish, his church equipment, or his salary. If one may judge from the sprightly talk when pastors get together for a "bull session," these things bulk large in their thinking.

In a way it is natural for a minister to think much about money. He may live in the midst of neighbors whose monthly income is larger than his year's salary. His wife mingles with women who think nothing of "hopping off" to England for a respite from the social whirl. His teen-age children go to school with boys who own "hot-rod" autos and with girls able to dress like daughters of Croesus. However saintly, the head of such a household is under pressure to "keep up with the Jones's." Year by year, especially in many suburbs, the pressure increases. To meet such demands the pastor feels that he must have more money.

A minister and his family ought to have a living wage, a comfortable home, modest insurance, and savings enough to educate the young folk. But when a pastor begins to think more about such things than about helping people to lay up treasures in heaven, he should beware lest he lose contentment and give way to covetousness (Matt. 6:19-34). In one of our largest states a responsible official, not a bishop, told me that among a thousand ministers under his general supervision at least 50 per cent felt dissatisfied with their lot, and usually because of a desire for more money. In one of those churches a leading layman said that the church would have given the pastor and his wife everything they wanted if they had not seemed so greedy, and demanded more than they earned.

In a community the pastor may look up longingly at the possessions of a few, and forget that the majority of the church members have smaller salaries than his own, and live in more modest houses. As with envy, a man singles out certain persons who have more than he, but does not feel sympathy for the many who have less. Whatever the facts in the case, few of us ministers are immune from covetousness. We live in a "sensate civilization" that seems to be money-mad, and we catch the contagion. Any such victim finds it hard to be on close terms with God, to engage in a spiritual ministry, and to keep growing in the likeness of Him who for our sakes became poor in things of this world, that we might become rich in the things of God (II Cor. 8:9).

The path of escape from covetousness calls for practicing what a man often preaches about being one of God's trustees. According to the first three Gospels our Lord said more about money than about almost anything else. When He spoke most clearly about the difference between Christian contentment and non-Christian covetousness he was addressing disciples, not least the future apostles. In time every one of them but Judas learned to trust God for the supply of all things needful in the ministry. As for Judas, a victim of increasing covetousness, even while in the apostolic band, no pastor wishes to claim his sort of "apostolic succession." The heart of the Sermon on the Mount (6:19-34) shows the folly of seeking first the possession of things that belong to others. Only the power of the Cross and the

Living Christ can set many a pastor free from this sin that prevails everywhere today.

Ministerial Sins That Seem Less Common

The four sins that follow seem to me less common among ministers today. Others may feel differently, and with cause. Amid all our "varieties of religious experience" each man has to look at such things through his own eyes, and from his own stance. The *Confessions* of Augustine, for example, stressed lust, one of these four "less common sins," which Bunyan did not stress in his two masterpieces, *Grace Abounding* and *Pilgrim's Progress*. At present I am following Bunyan rather than Augustine. Still I dare not ignore these "less common ministerial sins." I do not minimize the enormity of anger, for instance, but I think of it as often intermittent, whereas pride, envy, and covetousness tend to be habitual and most deadly.

Anger. Like most other sins, anger is the perversion of a God-like power. Without a capacity for God-like indignation no pastor could serve well as a spiritual leader of men. Once at Brighton, a seaside center of worldiness and sin, young Frederick W. Robertson watched a brute plotting to seduce an unsuspecting girl. The young minister was powerless to thwart that monstrous plot, but he felt such righteous indignation that he ground his teeth with what might otherwise have seemed like sinful rage.

When another man gets mad, anyone can tell whether or not he does wrong. As for oneself, it is a safe rule that my anger is always sinful. In his *Ethics* (IV, 5, 7) Aristotle long ago declared that men are angry for the wrong reasons, with the wrong people, in a wrong way, and for too long a time. Even if such exhibitions of ungodly anger did not dishonor God, and work havoc in the hearts of people nearby, such lack of Christian self-control would do untold harm to one's own soul. From every fit of unrighteous anger a minister emerges a less Christlike man.

Anger also works lasting harm in a man's body. Over in London the foremost medical man of his time was John Hunter. In lecturing about his specialty, diseases of the heart, he used to tell students that any man who dared to oppose John Hunter in an argument could make him so angry that he would drop dead. In due time he did die just that way. Now that lay church members are becoming increasingly concerned about health of body as a part of their religion, they feel that their minister should set them an example of Christian restraint. This feeling has to do with all four deadly sins that we deem secondary. In a minister each of the four involves a test of his self-control.

Strictly speaking, anger relates to an upsurge of ungodly feeling and an outbrust of sinful speech. In a minute or two a pastor can utter scorching words that go far to neutralize all the good he has done in pulpit and parish through years of faithful toil. From a worldly point of view, when he becomes known as unable to control his temper and his tongue, he may find it impossible to secure an opportunity to serve as a pastor. In such a "worldly point of view," where is the fallacy? I personally have incurred ill favor because I declined to recommend for an important post an able man who had publicly failed this way more than once. I refused reluctantly, because anger is one of my chief besetting sins. Who am I to judge?

Technically known as wrath, the same evil spirit may lead a minister to cherish permanent resentment. In class a man of this sort once told a roomful of other graduate students about his "friends" and his "enemies" among the lay officers. In as far as the rest of us could judge, the man's heart was full of bitterness and hatred. Most kindly one of the older ministers told him that a pastor ought to love every one of his officers and people. Even if some of them treated him shamefully, he ought to forgive, and go out of his way to win the friendship of any person aggrieved. What else does Paul mean by heaping "coals of fire on his head" (Rom. 12:20*c*)?

Lust. In the history of the Church a limited number of ministers have done untold harm by misuse of their procreative powers. Some of us have never felt strongly tempted to overt sins of this kind. If happily married, and discreet in the company of women and girls, a pastor can go through life without ever sensing the allurements of a siren. In Joseph's case the path of safety led to flight, but the deliverance really came through trust in God (Gen. 39:9, 12*b*). According to a golden promise about deliverance from temptation, God ever stands ready to "make a way of escape" (I Cor. 10:13).

Once I said something of the sort to a throng of seminary men who had asked me for counsel about matters of sex. Within the next six months three of the foremost Presbyterian pastors in a certain city had lost their ministerial standing because of proved adultery. Even so, I believe that for most of us the danger here lies chiefly in the heart. In his reading, thinking, and feeling, a pastor has to beware lest he offend by looking at a woman with lust. Before marriage he has to exercise control of thoughts and feelings. After he enters into wedlock, he may find to his amazement that it is more difficult than ever before to restrain his physical passions. Much as we Protestants believe in marriage of the clergy, we ought not to think of a marriage bed as a place for continuous indulgence of bodily passion.

Here again, the way of escape from sin comes through increase of love. A man who lives, moves, and has his being in the love of Christ on the Cross can think purely in the presence of any woman, and even control his appetite after he is married. This principle sounds forth in a widely known sermon that a pastor ought often to read: Thomas Chalmers on "The Expulsive Power of a New Affection" (I John 2:15).

Sloth, otherwise known as accidie, torpor, or downright laziness. Here again opinions differ about the prevalence of the sin. In his Cathedral novels Anthony Trollope gives the impression that clergymen are a lazy lot. Here at home one of the foremost

Methodist bishops speaks of laziness as the chief weakness of most pastors. In this judgment one of the best informed leading laymen of another denomination strongly concurs. My own experience with students and pastors leads me to another conclusion. I believe that many pastors who seem lazy suffer rather from the lack of a self-made plan, about which more will come later. If a minister suffers from planlessness, there is hope for him and his people. If from laziness, he ought to repent and reform, or else demit the ministry, which he disgraces. Away with drones!

For fuller light about laziness, read the Book of Proverbs, the only book in the Bible especially for a young man. Also, the Parables of our Lord. As for the cure, laziness drops away from a minister who falls in love with the Lord Jesus, with the people whom he serves, and with the ministry that he learns how to adorn.

Gluttony. As a kind of bodily intemperance gluttony often accompanies sloth. In early years a lad may form the habit of eating heartily because he works hard with his hands. Later in a sedentary calling he may not take enough physical exercise, but he continues to eat like a harvest hand, or a hardy horse. Once in a while, when invited out, a hearty meal can do no harm. But one a day ought to be enough, with two light repasts, thus allowing the stomach to recover. If invited to hold meetings for a week, a minister can ask that there be only one hearty meal, and that not close to the time of speaking.

Overeating, physicians say, is one of the prime factors in causing heart disease, and various circulatory disorders, which may in middle age issue in a stroke, or a coronary thrombosis. Excess of food also causes sluggishness of thinking, whereas the hourly work of a minister calls for clarity of thought, and ability to make wise decisions. Worse still, overeating shows the lack of self-control that belongs to the essence of Christianity. No person ever overeats to the glory of God. "The Kingdom of God does not mean food and drink, but righteousness and peace and joy in the Holy Spirit" (Rom. 14:17).

If you are a man given to appetite "put a knife to your throat" (Prov. 23:2). This kind of self-control pays rich and abiding spiritual returns. Many a minister would be a much better man, and far more efficient, if he regulated his daily intake of food and kept his weight down to normal for a man of his size. With a body that belongs to God, through the death of our Lord in a body, the man who dwells in that body can make it an effective agent of a soul that also belongs to God. With such a self-imposed regime more than one of us has enjoyed better health and more strength at seventy years than at twenty-five.

Not all seven of these deadly sins beset any one minister. Pride, envy, and covetousness appeal mightily to us ambitious folk who tend to live on our nerves, and on the nerves of everybody else. That takes nerve! Sloth and gluttony hold more sway over easy-going brethren. As for anger and lust, they roam somewhat at will, but chiefly among us who have restless spirits. Whatever a man's temperament, he ought to know which of the deadly sins keep him from growing more like the Sinless One. Then by the Spirit he can learn how to deal triumphantly with his besetting sins.

My soul, be on thy guard!
Ten thousand foes arise;
The hosts of sin are pressing hard
To draw thee from the skies.
—George Heath

Before a minister can hope to excel as a physician of souls he should put himself in the hands of the Beloved Physician. Instead of trying to deal with his pet sins one at a time, he may need for his soul a kind of blood infusion. When healing of soul comes from the Divine Physician, the minister will have abiding reasons for joy. Often he will give expression to his feelings in this majestic ascription of praise to the Most High:

> Unto him that is able to keep you from falling, and to present you faultless before the presence of his glory with exceeding joy, to the only wise God our Saviour, be glory and majesty, dominion and power, both now and ever. (Jude 24.)

CHAPTER XI

Personal Anxieties

PERSONAL ANXIETIES DIFFER FROM MINISTERIAL SINS. SINS HAVE to do with tendencies and desires always and everywhere evil. Anxieties of the sort in view relate to undue concern about things right and praiseworthy. The victim of one or more deadly sins may not be aware of his plight, but the man who feels anxious about things laudable knows that he is wretched where he wishes to rejoice. No one can judge the extent to which the seven deadly sins prevail in the hearts of clergymen who wish to become Christlike, but today one often hears about the ministry as "the perplexed profession." This does not mean that every pastor could qualify as a descendant of Martha with her domestic anxieties, but that such ministers seem to have been numerous of late.

In former times we thought about such things in terms of fear. The present tendency is to make a distinction between fear and anxiety, with more respect for the former. Today many informed writers agree with Karen Horney, a psychologist, in thinking of fear as "a reaction proportionate to danger," which is real, and of anxiety as "a disproportionate reaction to danger," which may be imaginary. "Any activity about which one feels anxious produces a feeling of strain, fatigue, or exhaustion." "Anxiety about a certain activity results in an impairment of that activity," and "spoils the pleasure it would otherwise hold." [1]

Without going further into the psychology of emotions, let us think about the effect on a pastor, religiously. Obviously,

[1] See Karen Horney, *The Neurotic Personality of Our Time* (New York: W. W. Norton, 1937), pp. 41, 57.

anxieties interfere with his relation to God. They tend to make it difficult for him to read the Bible, to pray, or to excel in any of the finer Christian graces, such as peace, hope, and joy. For much the same reasons anxiety, if at all chronic, interferes with a pastor's ministry among people. He serves in an era when countless folk seem bewildered and perplexed. Amid the same local conditions he ought to show how to live and work without feeling perturbed and overwhelmed. Otherwise how can he preach and pray about "the peace of God which passeth understanding," and counsel with a distraught friend who cannot sleep at night or sit still by day?

Anxiety takes its toll from a pastor's heart. It tends to weaken all his endeavors to become a more Christlike person, and it strengthens every tendency to pamper his weaker self. Instead of trying to confirm such statements by investigating the facts about other clergyman, a man has only to consult his own personal experience. When has he most surely grown in likeness to the God of peace, joy, and hope? When for a time he has felt most nearly free from carking cares. When has he most tended to slip into the ways of the world, the flesh, and the devil? When his heart has been most filled with anxieties about persons and things by no means base and foul. So that once again the things that matter most seem to lie at the mercy of those that seem not to matter much.

Causes of Anxiety

What causes a high-minded minister to feel anxious? Recently the Ministers Casualty Union employed an impartial opinion research bureau to ascertain statistically what troubles the pastors of our country. Through the replies to a questionnaire that went to clergymen all over the country, and in all sorts of churches, these experts arrived at certain conclusions, some of which now appear. To a friendly observer these findings show that the men in view seek for the advancement of the Kingdom through the local church, but that they seem to feel more concern about visible aspects of the Kingdom than about things that are unseen and eternal. In fact, so do we all tend to think these days.

In general, the pastor in view tends to feel much concern about the welfare of his family, his congregation, and his larger world. Many of his anxieties, though by no means all, have to do with "things that money can buy." If only to save time, we shall deal mainly with things financial. Among all the men who responded, 69 per cent expressed concern about ways and means of providing their sons and daughters with higher education. Even if more than 50 per cent of our pastors were not in debt, still it would be increasingly difficult for them to meet the rising costs of higher education, especially if two children go to college at the same time, and if one goes on for a costly degree in medicine.

Seventy-seven per cent of the pastors feel that they have insufficient funds for the purchase of theological books. Among the minority who receive budget allowance for such professional expenses, 59 per cent feel that it is not nearly large enough to meet the needs. This feeling about inadequate funds applies especially to the allowance for the upkeep of an automobile. (Locally our city allows a policeman nine cents a mile for the use of his car.) Sixty-two per cent of the pastors report that the amount received does not begin to meet the necessary outlay, which includes the cost of repairs, insurance, and depreciation. Concerning local equipment for church work, 45 per cent of the ministers who replied consider it inadequate; in the larger churches, 46.5 per cent.

Among all the churches represented, 52 per cent of the pastors voice concern about undue demands for administrative work; in churches with more than five hundred members, 58 per cent. In all sorts of fields 42.3 per cent express concern about the apathy of laymen. If it were feasible to conduct a similar study of opinions among laymen in these congregations, they might have something to say about the other side of these reciprocal relations. Meanwhile the fact remains that the ministers of America have abundant opportunity to feel anxious about "things that money can buy," and also about things that matter more for time and eternity.

Such a survey does not show that all the men who replied feel unduly concerned about "things that money can buy." Only God can tell how many or how few of us err in these respects. Still there can be no question about the reality of ministerial anxiety today. As for the causes, we ought to do everything possible to remove them, or at least mitigate them. Salaries ought to be larger, and allowances more liberal. But my own experience shows that a man's tendency to feel anxious about things does not decrease with a growing income. Among the pastors whom I know and love, the most contented ones are not rich, and the richest ones are not the most contented. By contentment I mean glad acceptance of one's lot as the gift of God, and daily endeavor to fill one's lot with roses. Something of the sort our Lord teaches in the heart of the Sermon on the Mount (Matt. 6:19-34).

I have a world of sympathy with pastors and their wives who worry. That has often been my main indoor occupation. I began with a salary of eight hundred dollars and the free use of a large manse hard to furnish and impossible to heat. I had to buy and maintain a horse and buggy. When I married neither of us had any financial backing or help from home. In later years the salary increased, but never so much as my desires. One of my seminary classmates told me that I was wasting my time in serving "student churches." "They fill up the pews, but do not help with the coal bills." As though that were the chief purpose of a church that touches the heart and minds of countless young folk on the threshold of life's adventure!

Gradually I discovered that my anxiety did not bring about any betterment in things external, and that it tended to unfit me for my ministry of "love, joy, peace, patience, kindness, goodness, faithfulness, gentleness, self-control" (Gal. 5:22). Take self-control. Who was I to tell others about living this way? Often I did not even try to curb my anxieties. When the children came to bless our home, I was in ill health. For a number of years I could not secure life insurance. I wondered how they could ever secure a college education, or how the household could keep its head above water. And so on! In those days I did not need anyone to tell me what makes a young minister feel anxious, or how such feelings interfere with his hours of devotion, his service among people, and his growth in Christlikeness. I was already too sorry for myself. What I needed was to dig down to the roots of this disorder in my soul. To be frank, I still am digging!

Light came to me through a sermon about "Anxious Care." In his early ministry Alexander Maclaren must have felt anxious about things, or he could not have dealt so understandingly with our Lord's teachings about Christian contentment. Singling out three places (Matt. 6:19-34) where the Master tells us believers, "Be not anxious," the interpreter points out the distinction between Christian foresight and ungodly anxiety. Out of the context he shows that forebodings are contrary to the teachings of nature, to the spirit of our religion, and to the workings of God's Providence. Toward the end comes a paragraph that shows the folly of anxiety, and also points out the path of escape. That was what I needed, and what many of my ministerial friends need now.

> What does your anxiety do? It does not empty tomorrow of its sorrows; but it empties today of its strength. It does not make you escape from your evil, but it makes you unfit to cope with it when it comes. It does not bless tomorrow, but it robs today. For every day has its own burden. Sufficient for each day is the evil that properly belongs to it. Do not add tomorrow's to today's. Do not drag the future into the present. . . . Fill the present with quiet faith, with patient waiting, with honest work, with wise reading of God's lessons of nature, of providence, and of grace, all of which say to

us, "Live in God's future, that the present may be bright; live in [God's] present that the future may be certain." [2]

Escape from Anxiety

This message from Maclaren helped me to see that the escape from anxiety comes to a minister by looking up to God through His Book, in the spirit of prayer. Like many a pastor today, I was doing things differently. I felt that if I could diagnose and describe all these symptoms they would disappear when exposed to the sunlight. But that way of self-treatment did not work. It merely made me all the more sorry for myself. That seems to have been the net result of our current way of dealing with others who feel anxious. We American ministers talk endlessly about anxiety, and yet we have the reputation of being the most anxious clergymen in the English-speaking world. In as far as I have found the way of escape from this disorder, it has come through forgetting about myself, looking up to God, and feeling concern about people in need of sympathy and soul help. In other words, I need to live by what I tell others when I counsel in private or from the pulpit.

1. *Philosophy*. Whether he knows it or not, every thinking man has a working philosophy. A minister can do no better than to accept the one in the key verse of the First Gospel: "Seek ye first the kingdom of God, and his righteousness; and all these things shall be added unto you" (Matt. 6:33). The context shows that "all these things" concern what money can buy. "Your heavenly Father knoweth that ye have need of all these things" (v. 32*b*). From Him a wise minister should learn to keep doing the will of God, gladly and well, and to trust Him for the supply of all the things that He counts needful. In this practical philosophy lies the Christian secret of serenity. Incidentally, despite my early anxieties, our children did get edu-

[2] See *Sermons Preached in Manchester*, first series (London: Macmillan, 1881), pp. 247-48.

cated, and their father lived to enjoy fifty years of active service in the ministry.

2. *Providence.* Maclaren rightly bases his pulpit counseling on the truth of God's Providence (Cf. Rom. 8:28). Here we need to think only about His loving care of one pastor and his household. For an object lesson of how faith in Providence sets a pastor and his wife free from anxieties, think of Spurgeon. After he got a good start at the London Tabernacle he raised money for vast projects, year after year, and he did so without difficulty or anxiety. Early in the ministry he learned to trust God for the provision of all the funds necessary in an expanding work that he felt called to do for the Kingdom. The facts that follow appear in his four-volume *Autobiography,* edited by his wife.

Spurgeon and his young bride had begun their married life with meager resources. Together they had agreed that they would not live beyond their means, or ever go in debt. One evening he came home feeling perturbed. "Wifey," he said, "I must give up hiring the horse, and walk to Park Street [Church, several miles distant] every time I preach." Somehow, perhaps for a relative, he had contracted an honorable debt of twenty pounds. His wife told him lovingly that it was impossible to quit hiring the horse. She begged him to do nothing about the matter until after they had prayed and slept. Then they laid the matter before the Lord. Here is the sequel, as reported by his wife:

"That night or the next day, I am not sure which, a letter was received, containing twenty pounds for our own use. We never knew who sent it, save that it came in answer to prayer. I do not remember ever afterwards seeing him painfully anxious for any of his great works. He depended wholly on the Lord, his trust was perfect, and he lacked nothing." [3] Incidentally, a man finds it far easier to live without financial anxiety if he has that sort of frugal wife, who prays.

[3] Chicago: Fleming H. Revell Co., 1898, II, 184.

3. *The Pastor.* This practical philosophy of relying on God's Providence relates to everything that concerns a minister, his family, his church, and his circle of ever-widening interests. As a servant of the Most High he knows that the responsibility for the work rests with God, and that He stands ready to guide in securing all the necessary resources. By grace and through faith a man learns to change conditions that ought to be changed, to accept those that he cannot change, and all the while to work in faith, without the sort of soul friction that we know as anxiety. Examples of the sort abound in the life of Hudson Taylor. Late in years he visited Australia. There a local clergyman asked him a question that concerns us all:

"You are occupied with millions; I with tens. Your letters are pressingly important; mine are of comparatively little moment. Yet I am worried and distressed while you are always calm. Do tell me what makes the difference."

"My dear M., the peace you speak of is in my case not a delightful privilege. It is a necessity. Without the peace of God which passeth understanding I could not possibly get through the work I have to do."

At another time Hudson Taylor received word of serious rioting and peril at two of his oldest stations, probably in China. Soon afterwards an associate heard him whistling the tune of a favorite Gospel song, "Jesus, I am resting, resting, in the joy of what Thou art." When the friend asked the older man how he could whistle while dear ones were in peril, Hudson Taylor replied:

"Would you have me anxious and troubled? That would not help them, and it would certainly incapacitate me for my work. I have just to roll my burden on the Lord."[4]

4. *The People.* In this practical philosophy the church officers and members ought to share, increasingly. As in any other family circle blessed of God, the practical work of a congregation ought to be a co-operative enterprise. This applies to money.

[4] *Op. cit.*, pp. 147, 159.

While the facts in the case may never be so simple as our books make them seem, the experience of many a "pastoral director" shows that the right sort of leader can get people to do and to give whatever they feel sure the Lord wishes them to do and give. Meanwhile, in a paraphrase of Carey's well-known words about Missions, a pastor with faith in God shows it by expecting great things from Him and His people; also, by attempting great things for Him and His people. Strange as it may seem, it is often easier to persuade them to do something hard and high than something little and low.

5. *Perseverance.* The most Godlike quality of a "pastoral director" may be perseverance. Some such practical philosophy as the one above must have strengthened and inspired two of the mightiest leaders in Bible days. Neither Isaiah nor Paul lived and worked in the midst of conditions free from occasions for anxiety, but each of them could write about God's perseverance. Herein lies the secret of prophetic assurance, of apostolic optimism, and of pastoral serenity:

> Hast thou not known? hast thou not heard, that the everlasting God, the Lord, the Creator of the ends of the earth, fainteth not, neither is weary? . . . They that wait upon the Lord shall renew their strength; they shall mount up with wings as eagles; they shall run, and not be weary; and they shall walk, and not faint. (Isa. 40:28, 31.)
>
> He who began a good work in you will bring it to completion at the day of Jesus Christ. (Phil. 1:6.)

CHAPTER XII

Outer Distractions

SOME OF US THINK MORE ABOUT DISTRACTIONS THAN ABOUT anxieties. We Americans live in an age of transition, confusion, and distraction. All these things belong together, as the antithesis of the spirit in which a minister can do his best work, and keep growing in Christlikeness. A hundred years ago there were five families on the farm to one in the city. Now the proportion has been reversed. Even in a remote rural area the spirit of a distracted city has begun to prevail. Except in an occasional congregation almost moribund, people tend to become bewildered. So does the minister. If all this seems extreme, listen to the questions from the floor at a conference of pastors. After an imported speaker has held up the ideals of this book, the discussion all has to do with distractions that prevent a minister from growing like his Lord.

How Ministers Have Been Distracted

There can be nothing new about the fact of outer distractions. They emerged in Bible days, as well as long afterward in a book that has received much attention of late, *Pastoral Care.*[1] Here Gregory the Great (d. 604) includes a chapter under this heading: "Preoccupation with the governing of others dissipates the concentration of the mind." Then follow these words, which many a pastor can verify: "Often it happens that when a man undertakes the cares of government, his heart is distracted with a diversity of things, and as his mind is divided among many

[1] Tr. by Henry Davis, S.J. (Westminster, Maryland: The Newman Press, 1955), p. 27.

things and becomes confused, he finds he is unfitted for any of them."

In more recent times the ablest all-round pastor among Presbyterians felt the effect of such distractions. In a rural field at Kilmany, Scotland, young Thomas Chalmers had found himself, spiritually. He had become a power in the community, and he had begun to be a saint. At the age of thirty-five he moved to a large and difficult parish in Glasgow. Soon he began to feel perplexed and bewildered by the multiplicity of demands on his time and energy. Because of those outer distractions he was losing his inward peace and imperiling his spiritual health.

After a year of vain attempts to deal with outer distractions he delivered a sermon about "The Christian Ministry Secularized" (Acts 6:4). First he surveyed the spiritual work to which God had called him as a pastor, and then he told about the other things that people in Glasgow expected him to do. While not in themselves wrong or needless, these things had little or nothing to do with what he felt he had been called of God to do in Glasgow:

> Were I to obey the call of these winged messengers, . . . then, my brethren, might I retire from the ministry of the Word and prayer altogether, and give not a single hour of the twelve month to the work of Sabbath preparation, and bid a stern refusal to every call of the sick and desolate and dying, and bid a final adieu to the whole business of family ministration. I might in this way, I assert, sink all that originally belonged to the office of minister of the Gospel, and yet earn the character among you of being a most laborious, hard-working, painstaking, and in a great variety of ways, a most serviceable minister.[2]

A week later Chalmers had intended to deliver a follow-up sermon, but he discovered that the lay leaders did not need any further light on this part of their responsibilities to God. They

[2] *Sermons of the Late Thomas Chalmers Illustrative of Different Stages in His Ministry* (New York: Harper & Brothers, 1849), pp. 367-68.

rallied to his support and used their collective wisdom in relieving him of surplus professional baggage. Thus they set him free for a ministry of the sort that he had envisioned. In a parish where the poor and the underprivileged abounded, that congregation did perhaps the best piece of community work in the history of our denomination. Meanwhile their "pastoral director" gladly gave himself to the special work for which he felt responsible to God. During all those years in Glasgow, after the first one of outer distraction and inner confusion, Chalmers kept growing in likeness to God and in power with men.

Since the days of Chalmers the outer distractions of a minister have vastly increased, especially here in the States. As a rule the pastor tends to blame the people, especially the lay officers, sometimes with just cause. Often the minister himself is largely at fault, or else his ecclesiastical superiors, who also have been ordained to the Gospel ministry. As for the laymen in many a church, they feel able and eager to set their pastor free from everything that prevents him from becoming a better man, a better pastor, a better leader in prayer, and a better preacher. They deplore everything that tends to distract him from the high calling of God. Here I speak about lay leaders in churches that I have known from the inside. Most of all, and kindly, they deplore ministerial unwillingness to share the work and the responsibility. In an occasional congregation worldly minded officers may wish to have a "live wire" or "go-getter."

All those "other things" about which Chalmers spoke needed to be done, and done well. In the days of the apostles at Jerusalem, needy widows had a valid claim on the congregation, and tables ought to have been served. But not by the apostles! In Glasgow other persons ought to have done all those things that young Chalmers attempted to do the first year. When their eyes were opened the lay leaders learned what the disciples ought to have learned when they assisted their Lord in feeding the five thousand (Mark 6:41-43) . In His "training of the twelve" Christ never did for others what others could do for Him. In a far different setting our own "park bench statesman," Bernard Baruch, accepted the headship of the Atomic Energy Commission. When he announced the names of his associates, he said with a smile, "You know that I never do anything myself." That was why he had time to sit on a park bench and think about big things for other men to do.

Everybody these days believes that the "pastoral director" ought to head an effective organization. But according to Samuel W. Blizzard, a statistical expert in sociology, a typical minister today devotes 50 per cent of his time and energy to "his" work as an executive. The majority of such pastors seem to feel that they have unwillingly become victims of our machine age, about which William H. Whyte has written ably in the book, *The Organization Man* (1956). Ministerial bondage to a machine age has come in part through "labor-saving devices," such as the telephone, the typewriter, the duplicating machine, the printing press, the automobile, and the airplane. In all these matters it is not easy to report the facts correctly. Even so, here is a case from a mission station in India. A saintly veteran is speaking.

> When I first came to Ceylon we traveled in bullock carts; now we travel in motor cars. The substitution of the one for the other has ruined our evangelistic work. Now I rush to a meeting and get back home. When I used to travel in a bullock cart I met people.

In commenting about this report from a missionary, D. T. Niles observes: "Hurry means that we gather impressions but have no experiences. We collect acquaintances but make no friends. We attend meetings but experience no encounter with God. If we are to find time we must encounter eternity." He says that in New Zealand he visited a volcanic region where he could envision a terrific outburst of molten lava. To his amazement he saw men and women calmly cooking meals with steam that escaped from crevices in the crater.[3] What a picture of our

[3] See Daniel Thambyrajah Niles, *The Preacher's Calling to Be Servant* (London: Lutterworth Press, 1959), p. 86. Not his ablest book.

world today! If a man of God knows what now lies beneath the surface of things, all ready to explode, who can wonder that he feels distracted?

What then can a busy pastor do to keep from feeling distracted? Later we shall consider practical ways of promoting ministerial serenity. At present let us think about a homemade philosophy, as a safeguard against pastoral distractions.

How to Keep From Feeling Distracted

1. *Admiration.* In the Bible and elsewhere a minister ought to admire busy leaders who seem never to have grown distracted. At a time when his entire world seemed ready to crash in, a man of faith once wrote: "Be still and know that I am God" (Ps. 46:10). When our Lord was on His way to restore the dying daughter of a centurion, He stopped to deal with a woman who had been chronically afflicted for twelve years (Mark 5:25-34). He seems always to have accepted interruptions gladly. In much the same spirit, when Augustine must have known that his home city was destined to fall, he wrote *The City of God* (c. 426), a majestic work, full of Christian serenity, assurance, and hope.

In modern times the Friends have shown us much about the meaning of serenity. They have taught us to sing, "Dear Lord and Father of mankind, forgive our foolish ways. . . . Take from our souls the strain and stress." A living Quaker writes about the secret of inner peace:

> The ancient doctrine of simplicity might be applied today to diminish the superfluous activities which prevent leisure and relaxation. The multiplicity of time-saving gadgets seems, paradoxically, to increase the general busyness and complexity of life. . . . The solution . . . is not to increase our attainments but to decrease our desires; in other words, to follow the path of simplicity.[4]

[4] See Howard Brinton, *Friends for 300 Years* (New York: Harper & Brothers, 1952), p. 143.

2. *Awareness.* A minister of a certain kind may not know that he needs deliverance from distractedness. He may have come from a home and a church, a college and a seminary, where people thought of Christian progress in terms of constant activity, like a merry-go-round with raucous "music." This kind of church life and work has become known abroad as "American activism." Christian activity has a large place in the life of a congregation and its minister, but so has Christlike repose, with "quiet seasons of the soul." There must be more or less of what we call church machinery, but machinery of the right sort runs so smoothly, so quietly, so inconspicuously that it calls no attention to itself. As for the man in charge, only when it breaks down does he have anything special to do with machinery.

Strange as it may seem, some churches run in this quiet way. The pastor seems never to suffer from hurry, worry, and flurry. He seems not to be distracted in doing his duty. And yet things get well done. After all, as Bushnell shows in his sermon about "Unconscious Influence," this is the way God works, and the way He wishes a pastor to work. Not "through the earthquake, wind, and fire," but through a voice of gentle stillness does God speak. Woe be to a minister if he cannot silence a noisy church machine enough to hear a whisper from heaven!

3. *Acceptance.* No matter how quiet and efficient the working of a church and a minister, distractions keep coming in from without. They will continue to do so until death. However, there is an old Chinese proverb that one can not keep birds from flying over one's head, but that one should not let them build a nest in one's hair. In other words, unwelcome interruptions and unexpected contingencies are sure to come. They should be accepted, even with an occasional crisis. In the heart where Christ lives there should be no feeling of resentment or annoyance. As Matthew Arnold sings in his "Lines Written in Kensington Garden,"

Calm Soul of all things! make it mine
To feel, amid the city's jar,
That there abides a peace of Thine,
Man did not make, and can not mar.

4. *Adjustments.* When a minister goes into a strange field he may expect a new set of outer distractions. Some of them he can mitigate or remove. A tactful note in the bulletin may request the people to help him reserve the morning hours for study, except in case of an emergency. A tactful wife or a secretary can intercept the majority of telephone calls, and would-be visitors. Soon the people will discover that they have in the study a minister who holds old-fashioned ideas about taking time to prepare for his work in public. As for an occasional neighbor who ignores such a request, he should learn that the minister's time is as precious as that of any physician or attorney. Such information soon makes the rounds through a "grapevine telephone" in the women's guild.

However, a new field has certain distractions that do not give way before tactful persistence. The roar of city streets and the customs of the community may interfere with the desired routine. Within broad limits a wise man accommodates himself to the new situation. Just as "God's weather never should interfere with God's work," so the external conditions in a field need not interfere with the minister's peace of mind and his ability to do first-class work. In the day's toil of a man well and strong, the body can accommodate itself to extremes of heat and cold. The Lord made the body so, and He can do much the same with a healthy soul. Not until a man goes home to God will he find a place free from distractions, but by adjusting himself to conditions here below he can enjoy much of heaven while he labors on earth. As Milton sings in *Paradise Lost* (I, 253-54),

The mind is its own place, and in itself
Can make a heav'n of hell, a hell of heav'n.

5. *Absorption.* Early in life every minister should learn to concentrate. Instead of requiring ideal conditions before he can do satisfactory work, a pastor can become so engrossed in his labors that he will not be diverted by outside distractions. When Paul wrote to the Philippians he was a prisoner in Rome, and yet he could declare: "I have learned how to be content wherever I am" (4:11*b*, Goodspeed). Largely because he had learned to accept outer conditions that he could not change, the apostle kept growing in Christlikeness. He concentrated on his work despite distractions.

Why all this concern about such a minor matter? Partly because a typical minister today suffers more from feelings of distraction than from most of the seven deadly sins. Somehow these lesser evils come into a man's soul to work havoc when the proper safeguards keep out the major evils. The little foxes spoil the vines (Cant. 2:15) that the wolves and the bears cannot reach. In other words, feelings of distractedness not only keep a minister from normal efficiency. They tend to interfere with his love for God and men. They also tend to injure or destroy the fruit of the Spirit in his soul (Gal. 5:22).

CHAPTER XIII

Pastoral Cowardice

A PASTOR'S FAILURE TO KEEP GROWING MAY BE DUE IN PART TO lack of courage. According to impartial experts, as we have seen, a typical pastor spends half his working hours on organization and administration. If so, wherein lies the fault? One expert lays the blame on "the demands of the congregation, the community, and the denomination." But who ever made a Protestant minister subject to demands that keep him from devoting enough time to his special work? Why does he not make a personal declaration of independence, and that for the remainder of his ministerial life? He need not bruit it abroad, or explain it to his people—at least not defiantly. But he can decide that he is the judge of how to do the will of God in expending time and energy. Such a stand calls for courage and "intestinal fortitude."

As a Bible example of such a declaration, this time in public, take Nehemiah. Knowing that "the good hand of God" was upon him, that leader of men relied on prayer to ascertain the will of his Lord. When others tried to divert him from doing his duty, the leader declared: "I am doing a great work and I can not come down" (Neh. 6:3*a*). In apostolic terms, "Where the Spirit of the Lord is, there is liberty" (II Cor. 3:17). Neither Paul nor Nehemiah thought of liberty in terms of license. Each of them stood out for liberty to do the will of God.

To carry out such a practical philosophy today calls for a vast deal of wisdom, tact, and courage. But when has it ever seemed easy and simple to refuse to conform? All the while there is a question about the extent of those "demands." Some of them may be imaginary. Personally I have never known a congregation or a community that went far in "demanding" that a pastor do this or that about the distribution of his time and energy. As for the denomination, there are certain reasonable expectations, but the official leaders whom I have known wish local pastors to spend much time and energy in ways spiritually productive. In general I feel that a minister should conform to the spiritual ideals of his denomination. I also believe that he should feel free to determine how he will lead the home people on to reach the desired goals. This takes courage. As a rule this means saying No to certain persons with plausible appeals.

Courage to Decide

Ideally, at the beginning of his active career, or even before, a minister ought to determine that he will devote the major portion of his time and strength to the things that matter most to God and the local church. When he comes to a new field, he ought to confer with those who know the facts, locally. Gradually he himself should decide what to stress during the coming pastorate. Serving under a bishop to whom he deferred, Brooks did something of the kind when he moved to Boston. According to the standard three-volume biography by A. V. G. Allen, Brooks had the courage to change his way of serving God as a local pastor. Largely giving up the sort of program that he had followed for ten years in Philadelphia, he devoted himself mainly to the study, the pastorate, and the pulpit, of course taking first-class care of the man in the case.

During twenty-two years at Trinity Church Brooks and his people enjoyed fruitful relations. He led in the removal to a more strategic site, and in the erection of a noble edifice. He also led in the raising of vast sums for Missions and other benevolences. Largely because of his pastoral ministry and his pulpit work Brooks exerted more of a nationwide and worldwide influence than any pastor in America today. And why? In as far as we can judge, because Brooks had the fortitude to map out his own course, and to follow his personal declaration of independence from the customs of clergymen who kept so "busy and troubled about many things" that they did not have time or serenity enough to seek and find "the one thing needful" in the eyes of God.

Since that time the pressure from without seems to have vastly increased. Today it requires far more courage to project and follow a self-made plan. But with courage and faith something of the kind is still feasible. In our day a Baptist minister comparatively young went into a field with all the customary "demands" from outsiders who strive to divert a pastor from his God-given tasks. After he had served long enough to know the needs and the "demands" he asked for a special meeting of the Board of Deacons, with the leaders of various societies. To those leaders of the congregational life and work he sincerely voiced his thanks for all they had done and were doing, Godward. Then he continued, somewhat as follows:

"Friends, you expect me to prepare and deliver good sermons." They all nodded assent. He proceeded to explain that he was not a genius, and that he had to work hard for what he got. Gradually he unfolded a self-made program for the distribution of his time and strength. In each case he noted that they all nodded assent. At last he paused, and then with a smile he asked, "How much of my time and strength do you think all of this will take?" For a while no one spoke, and then one of the most active deacons told him what they all felt: "We never thought of it this way before, but really what you have told us ought to take all your time and strength." Once again, they all nodded assent, most heartily. They loved and trusted their new "pastoral director."

Then he said, quietly, and with a smile, "Who is going to do the rest of the work around here?" At once they replied, through the same spokesman, "We will, if you let us!" Needless to say, he let them! Needless to say, also, the work of that congregation prospered, and the minister enjoyed all his years of service in that field. He gave himself wholeheartedly to the work that nobody but the pastor could do. This included over-all planning of activities among the lay workers. If there had been a supervising bishop, or district superintendent, he would have been delighted. With only an exception here and there, leaders of the kind whom I have known have been big men. Such men admire and encourage a pastor who leads his people to do big things for God. They also thank God if he has learned to say No to outside demands.

Courage to Be Different

Without being aware of cowardice, a pastor may abjectly conform to the ways of our "sensate civilization." Often it is the world, the flesh, and the devil—not the church, the community, and the denomination—that "demand" conformity to secularism. Years ago (1929 and 1937) two sociologists made series of studies in *Middletown,*[1] or Muncie, Indiana, a typical secondary city in the Middle West, where a pastor with a weak spine would scarcely know that he had a soul of his own. Here is part of a review of that book, and a word picture of such a community:

> In Middletown everybody is busy. Idleness is a vice.
>
> To be continually busy—to fill one's days with exacting engagements, to rush from one organized activity to another, to keep going—this is the supreme virtue in Middletown. . . . There is no time to read, no time to think, no time for those genial hours of irrelevance that make for serenity and balance. Instead everybody must justify his existence by doing something. . . . And one does these things because everybody else is doing them.

Of late this kind of secular pressure has increased. It appears in various books, notably in two by Vance Packard: *The Hidden Persuaders* (1957), and *The Status Seekers* (1959). These two books are secular, rather than religious. So is a clergyman secular if he conforms with all the expectations of what this writer terms a "packaged community," with its "custom-built" men,

[1] Robert S. Lynd *Middletown* (New York: Harcourt, Brace Co., 1929). *Middletown in Transition* (1937).

and its "other-directed person," it may be a parson, with a "packaged home," and a "packaged social life," "full of tensions, impatience, anger, and frustration." At first this may seem like a caricature, if not a farce. But it sounds strangely like the experience of a minister in a fashionable suburban community nearby. According to a friendly British observer of church life in the States, "The well-adjusted minister of a successful suburban congregation is in danger of forgetting that 'he has a responsibility to God as well as to his people.' " [2]

In *The Waste Land* (1922) and in other early poems, T. S. Eliot voiced increasing concern about modern "hollow men." In *A Man's Search for Himself* (1953) a well-known writer about counseling, Rollo May, refers to the chief problem of American society as "emptiness." He declares that freedom means "a man's capacity to take a hand in his own development." Under the guidance and the restraint of the Spirit a minister ought to assume the responsibility for his own life and service. In order to do so he ought to have an inner spirit like that of William Temple when he was inducted into a new and exacting work likely to distract him from the things of God. In his first address to the people whom he was to lead, Temple made a simple plea: "I come with one burning desire, . . . that we should help each other to fix our eyes on Jesus. . . . Pray for me chiefly that I may never let go of the unseen hand of the Lord Jesus and may live in daily fellowship with Him." [3]

Courage to Decline

Many a pastor would become a better man if he had courage to say No. Wholly apart from things questionable or wrong, he may attend too many meetings, some of them at a distance, when he ought to be at the home base engaged in his God-appointed

[2] See Daniel Jenkins, *The Protestant Ministry* (London: Faber and Faber, 1958), pp. 75, 76.

[3] See F. A. Iremonger, *William Temple* (London: Oxford University Press, 1948), p. 291.

tasks. He may work on too many committees, join too many societies, and make too many speeches or talks, some of which he has not taken time to prepare, and others on suggested subjects about which he cannot speak with knowledge or assurance. This habit of being ever busy about many things, mostly inconsequential, may carry over from the demands of college and seminary days. In school a popular student may feel obliged to conform with prevailing customs, no matter what the cost in the way of insufficient reading, thinking, and prayer.

At one time I served as pastor in a community where the leading Episcopal rector later became a bishop. Often I wondered how this man could lead in all the work of Trinity Church and still never seem hurried, worried, or flurried. In reply to such a question one day when we two were alone, he told me that after he had been on the field a while he had determined to lighten his daily load. Since he was a first-class mixer, especially with men, his personal declaration of independence called for a good deal of courage. At times the new self-imposed discipline must have seemed like taking up his cross (Matt. 16:24). But soon he began to witness the sort of parish harvest that the Lord has promised to the man who does intensive farming for God (Isa. 55:10-11). In substance he told me as a younger minister:

"When I first came to this capital city I felt flattered by being asked to make speeches and join clubs. Often I ran myself ragged by attending meetings that I did not think worth-while and by making talks that I had not time to prepare. Meanwhile the parish work was going back, and so was I. I was spreading myself thin, with constant outgo and little intake. In as far as I could see, none of those 'extra-curricular activities' ever helped to promote the worship, the work, and the influence of Trinity Church.

"Then I had the courage to reform. Soon I found that laymen could run the Chamber of Commerce and all the clubs in town, but that if I did not keep close to the life and work in my parish, nobody else could take my place." According to an English divine, the besetting sin of an urban clergyman today is "a futile and fussy multiplication of engagements which rather obscure than interpret spiritual duty. . . . He lives under the increasing pressure of obligations which fill his time, distract his mind, dissipate his interests, and hinder his reading and reflection." [4]

Testimony of a more intimate sort comes from "the Gloomy Dean," W. R. Inge. At the end of a busy year he wrote: "I sometimes fear that I am beginning to run dry. I preach too many old sermons and touch them up, and accept too many invitations. My devotional life is not what it should be; I do not meditate enough on the great things." Later he wrote: "Is it wise to accept most of the invitations that shower upon me? Is it wise to rush about all over the country, delivering for the most part old sermons and lectures, or addresses inadequately prepared? How often have I confessed that I was not satisfied with myself? . . . Have I been frittering away my time, and not allowing myself leisure to think earnestly and write carefully?" [5]

Courage to Delegate

On our side of the water lack of ministerial courage appears most often in executive and administrative work. Ideally, as leader of the home church a pastor guides in the formulation of wise plans—some of them far-sighted; in the selection of lay leaders to carry out these projects; in the over-all apportionment of the work so that everyone available has something worthwhile to do; and in securing resources sufficient to carry out the program. How much courage, tact, and perseverance all of this pastoral leadership requires no one can tell until he has had such experiences throughout a term of years.

The same principles apply in other fields of action. By turn-

[4] See Herbert H. Henson, *Retrospect on an Unimportant Life* (London: Oxford University Press, 1950), III, 15.

[5] *Diary of a Dean* (New York: The Macmillan Company, 1950), pp. 109, 153.

ing to such examples we ministers can see the basic facts, without professional bias. According to a first-class biography, the late Jan Smuts (d. 1950) of South Africa excelled first as a soldier and afterwards as a statesman. He might have attained much more distinction had he not suffered from two defects, not confined to South Africa. Smuts tended to deal with men brusquely, and he did not delegate enough work. "He imagined that nobody could do anything so well as he." [6] According to our most loyal and discerning laymen, the first defect is not uncommon among ministers, and the second is the chief weakness of the clergy. In both strictures I include myself when a pastor and as a professor.

Today an undergraduate seminary student may have charge of a church over the week end. There and in his first pastorate he may follow a succession of "short termers" who have not had time or ability to develop lay leaders. If so, the people may have become discouraged. As their easiest course of action the minister and his wife have formed the habit of doing many things more or less expertly. This custom they may continue throughout life, and far from joyously. While not always the case, such an experience is by no means uncommon. It makes one wish that we had a wise plan for providing every future pastor with a supervised internship for two or three years. In my own experience, after ordination it took three years of self-directed apprenticeship before I knew enough to be the "pastoral director" of a church. So I thank God for the Lutheran system of internship.

Whatever the reason, many a pastor does not delegate enough work to members of the salaried staff, which may at first include only a custodian and later a secretary, both of them on half time and half trained, but ready and willing to work. The failure to delegate work, responsibility, and authority appears more often in the pastor's dealings with the lay officers elected by the

[6] See F. S. Crafford, *Jan Smuts, A Biography* (New York: Doubleday, Doran & Co., 1943), p. 44.

congregation. These boards include persons with all sorts of gifts and graces, some of which the pastor may not possess. So do the leaders of the various organizations and societies, which select their own officers.

Together with the salaried workers, these lay leaders may constitute a sort of staff, or cabinet. Each of them likes to be treated as a person, not a thing; as an adult, not a child incapable of doing constructive and lasting work without being "bossed." If in an occasional church the lay officers and so-called leaders continue to show apathy, the blame may lie with the nominating committee in selecting the wrong persons. More often the fault rests with the pastor, or his predecessor. If once a minister "goes over the head" of a gifted person in charge of an important task or group, who can wonder if the "subordinate" loses enthusiasm and lets the "parson" keep the task that he has stolen? I know, because in those first three years I did wrong this way more than once.

Whatever the reason, a pastor may lack the vision to formulate a program that will call out the best in every potential leader or worker, and the courage to delegate authority and responsibility to go ahead without detailed instructions from the minister. The idea is not to manufacture jobs to keep skilled hands busy handing out church bulletins and dressing superfluous dolls. Neither is it wise to organize and continue needless societies. Late in life William Temple declared: "The Church is littered up with moribund societies that ought to have committed suicide gracefully years ago, but were perpetually being whipped up into a fictitious and frequently useless activity, either to satisfy the vanity of their committees or because some aged and faithful official had once served the society." [7]

In recent times the number of potential lay leaders has increased to a degree that augurs well for the morrow. People now live longer than of yore, and many of them retire. Even among

[7] *Op. cit.*, p. 276.

those who still work there is much leisure time which they stand ready to use in constructive ways suitable to their gifts. One such woman led in calling on newcomers in the community. Another became a sort of half-time unpaid pastor, with special concern for the sick, the shut-ins, and other persons in distress. A third led in the development and wise use of a church library on Missions.

A person who has recently retired may be ready for a large project much more daring. At Boston in Park Street Church a retired professor of law at Harvard assumed the leadership in a program of World Missions for which the congregation has become famous. To this layman the pastor ascribes much of the credit. Without knowing the facts from the inside, one feels reasonably sure that while the missionary program was going forward, the minister felt free to devote himself to work that the Lord did not wish him to delegate to laymen who were retired from secular activities and were now eager to work directly for the Church.

An example of a different sort comes from the Middle West. With one of the lay officers a pastor became much concerned about prayer. Gradually the two enlisted a group of laymen who met together at stated times to talk about prayer, and to pray. In their homes they began to read *A Serious Call* by William Law. In the resulting group discussions they agreed that the 1729 book had a message for today, but they felt that it ought to appear in a simpler form. So they decided that someone ought to abridge and edit the book, thus making it suitable for lay reading now.

The pastor himself could have done the work admirably. But somewhere along the line he had learned to share life's opportunities for constructive usefulness. As a consequence we now have in print a first-class book of devotions, abridged and edited in part by laymen.[8] While the book was in course of prepara-

[8] See *A Serious Call to a Devout and Holy Life,* ed. by John W. Meister (Philadelphia: Westminster Press, 1955).

tion the life and work of the home church seem to have flourished. No doubt the minister shared in the spiritual growth. Why so? Not least because he had led others to grow by using old-fashioned means of grace: food, spiritual fresh air, and soul exercise. The right sort of reading, the right sort of prayer, and the right sort of work—all under the right sort of ministerial leadership! What courage!

> That the leaders took the lead in Israel,
> that the people offered themselves willingly,
> Bless the Lord! (Judges 5:2 R.S.V.)

CHAPTER XIV

Continuous Tension

THE FOREGOING CONDITIONS MAY LEAD TO A STATE OF CONTINUOUS tension. The word here refers to an excess or abuse of what ought to be a normal part of ministerial life. Without something of the kind no one of us could lead aright in a prayer of adoration, officiate at a marriage, or do his part by an open grave. Professor T. B. Maston has written well about "Constructive Christian Tension," [1] but there can be nothing Christian or constructive about the sort of "strain and stress" that now appears under the heading of continuous tension. To be salutary, ministerial tension needs to be temporary.

Tension in the Light of Psychology

Tension ought not to continue until it becomes an inseparable part of a pastor's life and work. According to an old-time legend John once asked a huntsman why he kept his bow unstrung. The huntsman replied, "If I kept it always strung it would soon lose its spring." A pastor or a professor of the sort now in view takes himself and his duties too seriously. He does not know how to relax or play. He may not have a saving sense of humor, so as to see the absurdity of a mere man's trying to serve as Atlas, with the burden of the world resting on his shoulders.

No one but a psychologist could single out the various elements that enter into continuous tension. Whatever their number and identity they largely prevail in what the poet W. H. Auden terms "our age of anxiety." Placing myself among the

[1] See T. B. Maston, *Southwestern Journal of Theology* (Fort Worth, Texas, 1958), Vol. I, No. 1, pp. 21-29.

throng, I feel that in recent years the majority of the ministers I have known have suffered somewhat from this disorder of the nervous system, and that many of these victims have not been aware of their plight. This is no mere "children's disease," which a person tends to outgrow. Often the reverse holds true, so that increasing tension leads to stomach ulcers or a nervous breakdown. No pastor ever had either for the glory of God.

In our profession such ills often mark the work of an able man, high-minded and zealous. Fortunately, there is almost always a way to escape. Such a victory over continuous tension seems to have marked the prison experience of John Bunyan. In *Pilgrim's Progress,* which is largely autobiographical, the prose poet leads us into Doubting Castle, which is under the thralldom of Giant Despair. In the original edition this book presents ten reasons why a believer in Christ ought never to think of committing suicide. Together with the message about deliverance from Doubting Castle, through using the way known as Promise, this darkest part of the allegory ought to be more widely known. If it were it would raise a question: How did Bunyan ever learn so much about doubt, despondency, and the desire to die at his own hand? In prison he must have walked through such valleys with deepening shadows. If so, he came out into the sunlight of God.

This kind of knowledge comes through personal experience. In our own time a gifted author has told about his own continued tension, which led to a complete collapse early in his career. One need not agree with Harry Emerson Fosdick theologically in order to recognize his knowledge of psychology, his mastery of prose, and his courage in relating the facts about his nervous breakdown, with the specter of suicide. In his semi-psychological writings Fosdick has almost never revealed any secret of the confessional, but here is a worthy exception. He has been telling about his collapse while in the seminary:

Many times in later years I have faced people who started in to tell me the inner hell of their neurotic agony—the waves of melancholia, the obsessive anxieties, the desire for suicide and all the rest—and I have stopped them, saying: "Don't you tell me, let me tell you how you feel." One typical man, with wide eyes, exclaimed when I was through: "My God! how did you know all that?" [2]

Such glimpses over into the abyss ought to warn any clergyman about the peril of continuing in a state of tension. How then can he escape? In all matters that have to do with the unconscious, light may come in part from psychology. While not myself an expert in that field, I listen to masters with respect. Here I can do no better than quote one of them, and that with general approval. Since these ideas have become well known among pastors who read and think, I shall omit the author's comments, which seem to be for laymen, and add a few remarks for ministers. Incidentally, these psychological suggestions will help at times in dealing with other victims of continuous tension:

1. *Talk it out* (perhaps with a pastor).
2. *Escape for a while* (it may be in a call on the sick, a trip to the country, or a long vacation).
3. *Work off your anger* (or other ungodly feeling). The author suggests gardening, a game, or a walk.
4. *Give in occasionally.* (Why not often?)
5. *Do something for others.* (Lose sight of the "Big I.")
6. *Take one thing at a time.*
7. *Shun the "Superman" urge.* (Amen!)
8. *Go easy with criticism* (of others).
9. *Give the other fellow a break.*
10. *Make yourself available.*
11. *Schedule your recreation.*
12. *If you need help, get an expert.*[3]

[2] See *The Living of These Days, an Autobiography* (New York: Harper & Brothers, 1956), p. 73.

[3] See George S. Stevenson, M.D., *How to Deal with Your Tensions* (New York: National Association for Mental Health, 1958).

Tension in the Light of Religion

These counsels seem wholesome as far as they go. In my own nervous breakdown during late middle age I needed to go down deeper, and to look up higher. At a recent church assembly a prominent divine told young ministers that in view of such problems clergymen need "the basic philosophy of Freud, Jung, Adler, and James." Perhaps so, in part. "Depth psychology," for instance, coincides with Pauline teachings about "the mystery of iniquity" and "the stranglehold of sin." But when a helpless victim of continuous tension seeks for a way to escape from evils that well up out of the unconscious, he needs nothing less than the grace of Almighty God.

Whether a minister knows it or not, the chief cause of continuous tension may be sin. This view of things inward appears in a sermon by Brooks. He is preaching about Christ's gift of restfulness (Matt. 11:28-30). Gradually he leads up to sin as the basic cause of serious restlessness and other like spiritual disorders. "It is almost mockery to talk about everything else which Christ can do for man until we tell first what He can do for man's sins. If He cannot save the ship from wreck, it is a mockery to say that He can keep the cabins from disorder and keep the masts in place." [4] What then should a minister do about his own continuous tension? Here are some of the things he can learn to do:

1. *Recognize* the symptoms with reference to sin. If the facts call for a softer word, it may be infirmity, or shortcoming. By sin I mean any preventable "falling short" of what the Lord expects from a man in the way of character and performance. Friends with other ways of thinking prefer to employ the gentler terms. Whatever the label, no one of us should permit such a condition in himself to become chronic. Whenever a pastor

[4] See *The Law of Growth and Other Sermons* (New York: E. P. Dutton & Co., 1910), Vol. IX, p. 146.

feels so tense that he cannot work at even 50 per cent of his potential, he ought to blame himself, not his parents, his parishioners, his place in the world, or anything else that "gets on his nerves." After all, they are his own nerves, to control and to use as the gifts of God.

A certain pastor became so concerned about his bodily health that he consulted a physician who was not a churchman. The medical expert discovered that the clergyman's physical symptoms were due to his continuous tension, and told him that he could regain health of body if he began to follow the precepts he had been teaching others from the pulpit. Later when he reported to his wife, the minister broke down and wept. "To think that I, who have been preaching the gospel for years, should have to learn from an unbelieving doctor what my Lord tried to teach me before he was born!"

2. *Repent.* No softer word can tell how a clergyman ought to feel, and what he ought to do, when he becomes aware of his own chronic tension. By "living on his nerves" he has misrepresented God, failed to help people in quest of inner peace, and seriously impaired the health of his soul. He may not have made shipwreck of his ministry, but through maladjustment of inner forces he has wasted much of the God-given energy needful for his daily work. Before such a victim of chronic tension dares to preach about the forgiveness of the spectacular sins that beset other men, he ought to find deliverance from his own inconspicuous sins, or infirmities, which never appear on the statute books of men.

3. *Reform.* In our Master's teachings about the peril of an empty house (Matt. 12:43-45) He shows what a believer ought to do in his own soul. When once it gets free from evil demons it is not safe unless it becomes the abode of spirits that come from God. In terms of the New Testament this means having a heart filled with Christlike peace, love, and joy. "Whatsoever things are true . . . whatsoever things are pure, whatsoever things

are lovely . . . think on these things" (Phil. 4:8). Such counsels of "apostolic optimism" are as binding on a minister as on his lay friends. "The happiest person is the one who has the most interesting thoughts." In a hymn wedded to Sibelius' "Finlandia," Richard Watson Gilder leads us to sing:

> Through love to light! O wonderful the way
> That leads from darkness to the perfect day;
> From darkness and from sorrow of the night
> To morning that comes singing o'er the sea!
> Through love to light! O God, to Thee,
> Who art the Love of love, th' eternal Light of light!

Tension in Glad Retrospect

4. *Release.* Release from chronic tension may not come all at once. As a rule a person does not break the chains of habit overnight. Indeed the struggle may continue for years. Even so, the victory is sure if a man trusts in God. In as far as freedom comes it should lead to calm acceptance of sinless imperfection. Opinions may differ about the possibility and the fact of "sinless perfection," a term foreign to my own thinking. Really the phrase has arisen through various definitions of sin and perfection. There should be no question about the reality of sinless imperfection, both in the pastor and among those with whom he labors.

In writing to the Philippians the apostle assured them that he had not yet begun to attain perfection (3:12-16). He may have been thinking of his achievements, rather than his character. At any rate, if a pastor today wishes to enjoy the serenity that Paul showed in writing to his favorite congregation, the present-day leader of men ought to remember that neither he nor his people can attain perfection of performance. At the university a wise professor of English used to encourage us neophytes by saying that no person had ever written a page of perfect prose, and that he did not expect us to do so. What a way to escape from continuous tension! So if your endeavors fall short of the ideal, as they often do, and if the efforts of lay folk prove disappointing, as they often must, find solace in the fact of sinless imperfection!

5. *Rejoice*. When the Lord begins to set a pastor free from continuous tension, he ought to utter a daily prayer of thanksgiving. If his way of feeling taut has become a matter of habit, so will his new custom of feeling serene. After a minister has begun to rejoice in the divine expelling of these evil spirits, he can begin to share with others the Christian secret of contentment, peace, and joy, which come through being "in Christ." As every reader knows, these two words, "in Christ," sound the keynote of Philippians, "the epistle of joy" 4:4-7) . They show how the "God of peace" set His imprisoned servant free from inner stress and strain, so that he could do more work, better work, more joyous work, without worry, hurry, or fear.

On the contrary, the wrong sort of tension makes one think about excessive friction in a costly machine. For example, think about the making of Prussian blue, a ferrous compound widely used commercially in the manufacture of ink, paint, bluing, and dyes. In Berlin certain manufacturers once sought the counsel of Liebig (d. 1873) , the foremost living chemist. They wished him to tell them how to reduce their manufacturing costs, which seemed excessive. First they took him to the factory and tried to explain their processes. Soon he went away far enough to make himself heard. Then he asked why they did not tighten up their machines and keep them well lubricated. They replied that they had done so, and that they had begun to turn out an inferior product.

Then Liebig explained that in the manufacture of Prussian blue the most essential ingredient was iron. Instead of putting into the original compound a sufficient amount of crude iron ore, they were securing needful iron by wearing out costly machinery. In like manner Charles Lamb once wrote a "Dissertation on Roast Pig." There he showed, quite whimsically, that a man does not need to burn down his abode in order to enjoy the succulence of roast pig. If that long-suffering machinery or that abused building could have cried out in protest, either of them might have exclaimed: "What fools these mortals be!" So Elizabeth Cheney sings about what she "Overheard in an Orchard:

> Said the Robin to the Sparrow:
> "I should really like to know
> Why these anxious human beings
> Rush about and worry so."
>
> Said the Sparrow to the Robin:
> "Friend, I think that it must be
> That they have no heavenly Father
> Such as cares for you and me."

Fortunately, more than a few ministers and missionaries have learned how to live happily and work hard without continuous tension. Testimony of the sort comes from one of our foremost nuclear physicists, Arthur H. Compton, winner of the Nobel Prize. He refers to his father and mother, as well as his sister, the wife of a missionary to India. In reply to a native government official, who had spoken about our American "sense of lostness and our tensions," the Christian man of science told about "the lives of those whom I have known best, the glow on the faces of those who have truly loved others and have spent their lives in enabling others to live more fully." [5] Such inner peace and lack of continuous tension come to a believing heart as beautiful tokens of the Father's love.

[5] See *Atomic Quest, a Personal Narrative* (New York: Oxford Press, 1956), p. 336.

The peace of God, which passeth all understanding, keep your hearts and minds in the knowledge and love of God, and of His Son Jesus Christ our Lord. And the blessing of God Almighty, the Father, the Son, and the Spirit, be amongst you and remain with you always. Amen.

CHAPTER XV

Chronic Immaturity

A PASTOR'S INABILITY TO COPE WITH OBSTACLES MAY BE DUE TO chronic immaturity. According to Harry A. Overstreet, "A man is at his best when he is doing his best at what he can do best. . . . It is the business of a man to keep maturing throughout his life, along the line of what in him is unique, and what he wholesomely shares with others." [1] From this point of view let us think about the life and work of a typical young minister. We shall assume that he is called of God, properly trained, and eager for a career of increasing usefulness. We shall begin with him after ordination at the age of twenty-five. Then we shall look at four successive stages, with suggested time limits more or less arbitrary.

I. Years Full of Promise (25-40)

Everyone concerned ought to look on such a young minister with favor. In our time more than in others we tend to idealize youth as the golden age, and as a rule we do well. In the Church we welcome a young clergyman with all his charm and promise. But we do not always deal with him wisely. We seem to forget that many a young seminary graduate is still ministerially immature. Instead of requiring a year or two of supervised apprenticeship, as with a would-be physician, we immediately put an inexperienced minister in charge of a congregation with a score of organizations and with twice that many perplexing problems. We seem not to know that it requires more ability to direct the activities of a comparatively small "problem church" than to keep things going forward in a larger congregation where

[1] See *The Mature Mind* (New York: W. W. Norton & Co., 1949), p. 41.

talented lay leaders have worked together harmoniously in seeking first the Kingdom of God.

Strange to tell, many a young pastor meets every early test and comes through without a sense of frustration. He can do so most surely if he discovers that he is not yet ministerially mature. With all his robust manhood and personal charm, he cannot do best what he ought to do best. Like young Henry Ward Beecher, and many of us not at all famous, the young pastor needs to learn what to preach today, and how to do it well, week after week; how to lead in public prayer, and get the people to pray; how to plan the work, and then get it done by lay workers full of zest. He may not know the hearts of ordinary people, and how to meet their needs as pastor and counselor. Neither may he know enough theology and ethics, or enough of the Bible, to put a lasting foundation under these first few years of adventure into the unknown spiritual world.

The young man in view survives, and keeps maturing. He has humility and tact in all human relations. He finds that the people love him and do not expect from him the practical wisdom of a mature minister. For some reason, however, the first pastorate does not usually continue so long as later ones, which may well average about ten years. In the second field the growing minister may discover that by trial and error he has engaged in a self-directed apprenticeship. Thus he may have learned what he ought to have known before he was catapulted into a work beyond the present powers of many a seminary graduate.

After these first few years of experiment in the most difficult professional work on earth, a pastor may blame the practical department of the divinity school. If so, he may forget how little time the overcrowded curriculum allows for things supposedly unscholarly because down to earth. Of late, however, the custom of assigning an undergraduate student to a part-time field tends to alter the situation. It usually does so by depriving him of an opportunity to become educated through long hours of quiet reading and study, all of it unhurried. With twice as many subjects as his grandfather studied in the seminary, the young man devotes to his books about half as many working hours. On the contrary, a medical student does not enter into active practice "on his own" until he has completed five or six years of preparation after college.

Despite our lack of wisdom in providing for the adequate training of future pastors, in most cases that I have known the young men have kept maturing admirably. Before he comes to the age of forty many a minister has already fulfilled his early promise, and is ready to keep going on for thirty years more of ministerial growth. On the other hand, a leading divine in Britain has told about a gifted young clergyman who failed to mature with age. Unlike the apostle (I Cor. 13:11 *a*), this young fellow failed to put away childish things. In middle age "he had much of the charm which attaches to the reckless impulsiveness of an eager and affectionate boy. But he lacked the less attractive qualities of an administrator, a teacher, and a judge. . . . He evoked much personal affection and yet he commanded little influence and he wielded little authority." [2] Whether he knows it or not, when such a "good fellow" has reached the age of forty, he probably has passed the crest of his usefulness.

Unless a young minister keeps improving in heart and life, he soon begins to slip back. At the age of forty a pastor may have lost much of his early appeal. If so, what does he have to take its place? Does he not know that the laymen called him because of the promise that he has not begun to fulfill? In an extreme case, by no means unheard of, a pastor at the age of forty knows less about the Bible and other books, and less about men, than he knew at twenty-five. He may not preach and pray so well, partly because he has not mentally kept pace with a world that has been swiftly changing. He may have kept free from adultery and the other glaring sins about which we rightly warned him

[2] See H. H. Henson, *Retrospect of an Unimportant Life* (London: Oxford University Press, 1950), Vol. III, p. 321.

in seminary days. But has he employed the God-given means that would have insured the growth of his inner being?

In view of such possible immaturity at the age of forty, what should an older friend say to a young seminary graduate, richly gifted and full of promise? Here follows the heart of what I have learned by watching young pastors who have kept maturing, and by reading the lives of others who have made a wise use of their opportunities to grow more like their Lord:

In the beauty of your ministerial morning set up ideals so lofty that you will never need to change them, except as they keep soaring higher. During these habit-forming years so live and work that when at last you retire you will feel glad that you have lived and worked this way. Form working habits that you will never need to alter, except as new conditions call for different ways of doing the same grand old things for God. Above all, live and work in the spirit of Christian love. After you have learned how to handle your ministerial tools, you will find that you can do well whatever you enjoy doing for God, and that you can learn to enjoy doing for Him whatever you keep doing well. So in dealing with people, if you love God supremely, you will love them largely, and they will love you increasingly. In the spirit of Christian love, both you and they will continue to grow in likeness to your Lord.

II. A Period of Transition (40-55)

In the pastorate, ideally, middle age ought to be full of constructive achievement, attended by continuous growth. In the legal profession, as in other learned callings, a man normally expects to keep maturing throughout middle age. But in the ministry the reverse often holds true. During the first fifteen years or so a man keeps on toiling with all his might, and developing according to the expectations of his admirers. All the while he has kept buoyed up by hopes of advancement to a larger place in the sun. But in the early forties he may figure out that he has gone as far up as he will ever go. Then he may wonder why coveted positions keep going to younger men, less mature. Partly for such reasons, more ministers seem to make shipwreck, or get stranded, during middle age than at any other period. Much as we talk and think about the perils of a young clergyman, we ought to feel more concern about "the destruction that wasteth at noonday."

There can be nothing new about the appearance of unexpected pitfalls during middle age. In earlier history at which stage of life were men of ability and promise most likely to fall down? Roughly speaking, between the ages of forty and fifty-five. In Bible days think of three strong men whose lives overlapped: Saul, David, and Solomon. In the Parables look at the Elder Brother, Dives, and the other Rich Fool. Among Shakespeare's tragedies, consider Othello, Macbeth, Hamlet's uncle, and King Lear's two older daughters. As for biography and fiction, space does not permit a listing of casualties in middle age. Whimsically, P. G. Wodehouse says about men in "the middle passage of the years": "Time like an ever-rolling stream bears all their charms away, so that the good chap of twenty becomes the stinker of fifty."

Here the humorist starts with an echo of a first-class hymn and ends with a descent into malodorous prose. Thus he suggests a contrast between the beauty of a ministerial morning and the lack of appeal in the "same" person's middle age. He has not become a "stinker," but still he deserves our sympathy. As a victim of forces apparently beyond his control he has suffered a loss of early idealism and hope. He may have become a cynic; as Browning would say, a clod, "untroubled by a spark." Instead of receiving from his alma mater a coveted D.D., he may qualify for a sort of double D.D., as an example of Disillusion and Discouragement, Despondency and Despair. In an extreme case he suffers a nervous breakdown and tries to commit self-murder. Even if he regains full mental health, his pastoral concerns may have lost much of their luster, and his spoken word much of its sparkle. "The bird with the broken pinion never soared [so] high again."

Such a word picture may seem too dark, and even hopeless. Even so, it will serve in contrast with what here follows. Across the portals of late middle age no man of God ought ever to behold the words of Dante about the place of perdition: "Abandon hope, all ye who enter here"! In middle age, after a time of disillusionment and despair, by the grace of God a minister past fifty can right himself and then keep going on to the most fruitful and blessed portion of his entire career. If during the perilous years of middle life he "finds himself" anew, because he has rediscovered God, he can get his "second wind," and then keep on maturing until he retires. This does not mean that he will have a succession of important charges, each of them "bigger and better" than the last. The Church will not soon abandon its custom of giving such places to men before the age of forty. In the Providence of God a minister's opportunity to keep growing in spiritual stature does not depend on the bigness and the bluster of a "popular pulpit" on Broadway.

For a Bible example of a powerful man who in middle age temporarily gave way to despair, turn to Elijah (I Kings 19). All through his earlier years, we assume, he kept growing in power with God and with men. At last on Mount Carmel he won a mighty victory for the Kingdom. Then he entered into a period of disillusionment and despondency, with a strong desire to die. If that mood had become chronic, Elijah would not afterward have dared to face cruel King Ahab, and rebuke him for his sins (I Kings 21). Neither would the prophet still later have stood with Moses on the Mount of Transfiguration, there to represent "the old-time religion" at its noblest and best. As we often say, "What a comeback!" We ought rather to say, with wonder and awe, "What hath God wrought!" See what He can do in the heart of a man who in middle age seemed to be on the way "down and out"!

In passing let us note that much the same pitfalls await many a layman in his middle years. In my experience as a pastor and counselor I have witnessed a larger number of casualties in this age group than among young folk who come to church. And yet I have never heard from anyone but myself a sermon or a prayer that revealed strong concern for the spiritual welfare of persons in middle age. In a typical house of worship today the men and women between forty and fifty-five may outnumber all the others present. They may also be spiritually the most needy.

With all our commendable zeal for young people, and all our concern about their temptations, why do we ministers practically ignore their fathers and mothers, especially when they are striving to keep from being submerged in what Helen Keller terms the "midstream" of life? Can we not open to our middle-aged friends a door of hope in God? On this whole subject I may seem to be unduly sensitive. If so, I can only plead that in late middle age I suffered a complete nervous breakdown, which for a while threatened to stop my ministerial career. Since that time, I have had strength to write my books for ministers, and to serve God in various churches, largely among men and women neither young nor old.

III. A Time of Fruition (55-70)

> Grow old along with me!
> The best is yet to be,
> The last of life, for which the first was made!
> Our times are in His hand
> Who saith, "A whole I planned,
> Youth shows but half; trust God, see all, nor be afraid!"

These well-known lines from Browning's "Rabbi Ben Ezra" may well serve as a motto for a pastor when he draws near to old age. Really, a man need seem no older than he feels, but at each successive period of life he ought to act his age. If he has accepted Browning's practical philosophy of Christian optimism, a minister can keep on feeling young in heart. This working philosophy of hope rings out in the later stanzas of "Rabbi Ben Ezra," and elsewhere in Browning's poems. While often far from easy to read and comprehend, this man's poems bring a pastor more of uplift and strength than those of any other English-speaking bard. In full view of life and its "tragic sense," Browning bids a man look up, not down; forward, not backward; and keep moving onward, with full assurance of God's favor. For example, consider this insight from Browning's masterpiece, *The Ring and the Book* (1868-69), which he completed when fifty-seven years of age:

> Years make men restless—they needs must spy
> Some certainty, some sort of end assured,
> Some sparkle, though from beacon-tip,
> That warrants life a harbor through the haze.

The closing years of a full-time ministry ought to prove the most fruitful of all, and the most joyous. The field may not be so wide as the one in middle life, and the statistical reports may not seem so impressive. But as a man grows older and more Christlike, he learns not to judge a church or its pastor by what he can see on the outside. This point of view appears in the latter part of a light novel by Agnes Sligh Turnbull. As in her other stories she does not write about the mud in the Main Street of "Ladykirk." But she does show an understanding of how an elderly village pastor can keep growing more like his Lord.

In *The Gown of Glory* everything centers around David Lyall. Somehow he never could "rise above" his lowly station as the pastor of an inconspicuous village church. In early years he shared his wife's dreams about being transferred to "a larger work." But time after time the doorway failed to open into a "better church." Gradually he learned how to find peace of heart, contentment, and joy in his little appointed lot. Here follow some of the closing words in this pleasing tale about a gifted minister who never seemed great. The paragraph relates to an aging pastor before he retires:

> He had never known such peace. It was different from any passing elation or transitory content. He could even think now of the confident young man of dreams who had first come to the manse. He could remember without wistfulness or regret, for the old sense of inadequacy and failure had left him. He knew that he had done his best work in the place to which it had pleased God to call him. While his feet had traveled the uneven flagstones of Ladykirk, his soul too had journeyed.[3]

IV. Days of Retirement (70-85)

"The last of life, for which the first was made!" These words from "Rabbi Ben Ezra" should hold true of every minister who has come past the age of compulsory retirement. For most of us that means seventy. The Methodist Church allows a minister to retire at the age of sixty-five and he must do so at seventy-two. Either way, normally, he receives a pension for the rest of his life. Many of us who have passed these age limits feel that some such requirements are expedient. Both for his own sake and for the sake of the congregation, an oldster ought to be released from full-time service. During his remaining years, and those of his widow, the Church at large ought to provide a pension sufficient to insure comfort and freedom from care.

But retirement ought not to involve compulsory inactivity. Idle hands soon become shaky, and unused powers quickly wane. According to *Today's Health,* an excellent popular monthly journal sponsored by the American Medical Association, "The fatigue of older persons is seen most commonly among persons who do not have enough to do. Too often they

[3] Houghton Mifflin Company, Boston, 1952, p. 402.

feel that their life work is done. Their fatigue has its origin in boredom and loss of interest and incentive. Over and over again, when a crisis arises, or something of deep interest comes along, these individuals lose their fatigue."

A retired minister can usually find something worthwhile to do. Without embarrassment to his successor in the pastorate, and without depriving any younger minister of an opportunity to work full time, a retired pastor can keep on exercising his spiritual muscles. In Washington, D.C., a clergyman impressed physicians and others by his ministry to the sick. Since retirement he serves as the unpaid Protestant chaplain of a city hospital. In days to come, let us hope, the Church will show much concern about providing such a veteran with something useful to do. But as a rule each man has to discover his own field of post-pastoral service.

Much the same principle applies to other callings. In the promotion of classical learning, for instance, Edith Hamilton still keeps active after the age of ninety. In Athens recently she witnessed a performance of *Prometheus,* which she had translated into English. On the way to that noteworthy spectacle she told her friends: "The happiest decade is between eighty and ninety. You are more free of yourself."

As a crowning example of one who kept maturing in later years, turn again to the apostle Paul. In his letter to the young church at Philippi he tells about being "in the Lord" as the secret of continued growth in Christlikeness. In the heart of this letter about Christian joy he writes a few words that could well serve as a motto for this chapter, and this book. Remember that he is writing from prison:

> One thing I do, forgetting what lies behind, and straining forward to what lies ahead, I press on toward the goal for the prize of the upward call of God in Christ Jesus. Let those of us who are mature be thus minded." (Phil 3:13*b*-15*a* R.S.V.)

CHAPTER XVI

Inadequate Planning

ALL THE UNFAVORABLE FACTORS SO FAR MAY IN LARGE MEASURE be due to lack of foresight and system. Much the same conditions obtain in other fields. At a mass convention in Canada the head of a large corporation told about a business that had kept going back, no one knew why. At last the governing board called in an efficiency expert, who made an investigation into the working methods of the various executives. After he had conferred at length with each official the expert told the President that the fault lay chiefly with him as the head. Among the staff he had become known as a tireless worker, an inveterate worrier, a penny-pincher, and a procrastinator, unable to make a decision, and unwilling to delegate responsibility.

At first the President insisted on resigning. He had gradually lost all confidence in himself, and in his ability to command the respect of the other officials. Reluctantly he consented to continue as chief, but on a new basis. With the requisite assistance he would begin at once to plan the work of the corporation. Then he would make clear to each official what his department was expected to do, leaving him free to follow methods of his own devising, but holding him responsible for the results. Thus the President would arrange for other men to deal with all matters except the relatively few that demanded the attention of the chief executive.

Almost immediately the business of that corporation began to look up. Soon it regained its former position of leadership, and then it stood ready to forge ahead. Near the end of this absorbing address the speaker explained that he had been the culprit. After his change of outlook and attitude the other officials to a man rallied to his support. They entered into their respective assignments with new assurance and enthusiasm. Now that the chief executive desk no longer served as a bottleneck for countless things large and small, he could devote his time and energies to over-all planning, and to making vital decisions.[1]

Division of Labor

This recital may sound like a present-day version of what Moses once learned from an older man about "division of labor" (Exod. 18:13-26). Indeed, the idea of planned activity appears repeatedly in Holy Writ, not least in the Book of Proverbs and in the Parables of our Lord. A helpful book [2] about the human aspects of His ministry shows that the Parables often stress such old-fashioned virtues as foresight and system, industry and thrift, liberality and other traits that we often ignore. In His "training of the twelve" our Lord often employed parables and other teaching devices which show future church leaders how to carry on their work for the Kingdom. In setting forth lofty ideals He approved the faithful steward, or trustee, who planned his work with care and then carried out his plans with zeal.

The bearing on the life and work of a minister appears in a work by another evangelical liberal of yesterday. In his Yale Lectures Charles E. Jefferson spoke about *The Building of the Church.* Two excerpts will show how this book helped me as a young pastor, when I felt confused because of general planlessness. Fortunately, Jefferson did not go into detail far enough to prevent me from working out plans that suited me personally, as well as the conditions in my field. Somehow he made me see what the Lord meant by sitting down to plan before one rises up to build:

[1] For the facts see Ernest Havemann, *The Age of Psychology* (New York: Simon & Schuster, 1957), Chap. X.

[2] See T. R. Glover, *The Jesus of History* (New York: Association Press, 1917), p. 130.

There are two sorts of ministers whose careers are tragic. The first are those who do not see clearly what it is that they are to do. . . . They walk like men in a fog. The second see with some degree of clearness the destination, but they are too careless or precipitate to build the agencies by which the goal can be attained. Both classes of men arrive nowhere, the first because they do not know where they want to go, the second because they lack the wisdom of fitting means to ends. . . .

A church likes to feel itself in the grip of a man who knows where he is going. Nothing is so discouraging to Christian people as to feel that their leader is not leading. The outlook is indeed dark if the [minister] does not know what he and his church ought to bring to pass. Simply to keep the church machinery running for the sake of seeing the wheels go round is a vexation of the spirit. . . . "Vanity of vanities, all is vanity!" A minister has not made the highest possible use of his [annual] vacation unless he comes out of it with a plan for the next year's work. . . . A definite and well-considered plan is a minister's life preserver.[3]

About all these matters in terms of today H. Richard Niebuhr has written an able book, *The Purpose of the Church and Its Ministry*.[4] After an exhaustive study of current theological education, Niebuhr and his colleagues have sent out this volume and two others, with special reference to the training of "pastoral directors" for tomorrow. In view of these current proposals, and on the basis of principles in the Scriptures, every pastor ought to formulate a practical philosophy for his life work, and a workable program for his leadership of the home church, especially during the next year. Such an over-all plan for one's ministry as a whole, and for the coming year, may be so simple that it scarcely needs to appear on paper. Still it can do no harm to write it out and keep it at hand for reference whenever the fire burns low in one's heart.

[3] The Macmillan Co., New York, 1913, pp. 233, 241 (o.p.)
[4] Harper & Brothers, 1956.

We can not kindle when we will
The fire which in the heart resides;
The spirit bloweth and is still,
In mystery our soul abides,
  But tasks in hours of insight willed
  Can be through hours of gloom fulfilled.[5]

Plans in Mid Summer

In view of such long-range ideals a pastor may set apart during his mid-summer vacation an hour a day for planning a year's program. For some reason, Brooks used to say, the work of a local church begins in the autumn. It may well be when the public schools open in September. Even if the home church does not follow the Christian Year in matters of worship, the pastor may employ its general principles to guide in his over-all planning. Then the year may fall into four parts, known here as "quarters," though they are not equal in length. The first one extends through the fall and culminates at Christmas. The second runs through the winter and reaches a climax at Easter. The third includes the months of spring. The fourth covers the summer time. Unfortunately, neither of these last two seasons may have a climactic goal. Herein lies perhaps the chief difficulty in planning by the "quarter." How can one prevent a gradual slowing down after Easter, and a decided slump in summer?

A more difficult way of planning uses the month as the unit of time. At first glance this method seems somewhat arbitrary. During the fall, for instance, anyone can see the wisdom of leading up to Thanksgiving, and beyond that to Christmas. But in what vital respect does October differ from September? In practice, however, the plan usually works unexpectedly well. Out on the farm men plan by seasons. In the city they employ the month as a time unit. So they find it easy to work with a minister who plans by the month, each time, ideally, with some-

[5] From "Mortality" by Matthew Arnold.

thing new. In fact, there can be no way in which a minister plans intelligently without reaping benefits, both for the people and for himself, not least in peace of mind.

Let us think about a case, more or less typical. After Easter a man forty years of age comes into a field new to him. Before the end of July he visits the people in their homes and mingles with them in various groups. He also confers with the elected officers and with other lay leaders. Gradually he sizes up the local situation, which calls for a program different from that in his preceding field. During a midsummer vacation he gets far enough away to see the new work as a whole. Then he plans broadly for the worship, the teaching, and the work of the congregation, in as far as it relates to him as the responsible leader. With the quarter as the unit, or else with the month, he plans for the year as a whole, and more in detail for the first main unit of the approaching season. In all this planning he aims not to impose any schemes on the people, but to lead them in doing what their lay leaders desire for the local church.

When he comes home he requests the proper lay officials to arrange for a planning conference. Preferably at a distance from the church the lay leaders of the various boards and organizations come together with him for a spiritual retreat, issuing in a free-for-all conference, with happy fellowship at one or two meals. From such a retreat everyone present ought to come away with a clear understanding of what the local church aims to accomplish during the coming year. Each person ought also to know what his own committee, board, or society should plan to do for the common good. In short, this kind of "pastoral director" aims not to become a dictator or a slave driver but a co-ordinator and an inspirer. To a certain extent he may resemble the right sort of baseball coach. He does not take an active part in any game, but still he leads the team to many a victory.

In his own part of the work a minister ought to set others an example of quiet and efficient activity. "Let everything be done decently and in order." Such an ideal calls for ministerial foresight, system, thrift of time, and generosity, as well as "effortless mastery" of all the work the Lord has given a man to do. With a master plan for the year, and perhaps for a number of years, and a more detailed program for the next quarter or month, he ought to have a schedule for the week, and for each day. Ideally, a working day should include no "unscheduled hours." As for interruptions sure to come, it is easier to "take them in stride" if a man knows where he is going and how he expects to get there. For an example of such "effortless activity" study a scene in the life of our Lord (Mark 5:22-43). Note how He accepted interruptions while in pursuance of His plan.

All of this may seem too general. If so, the reason is that no book or cliff-dwelling "expert" can tell any local pastor how to use the resources at hand to meet the needs of the community during the coming year. But the Lord knows, and He stands ready to guide. "If any man will do his will, he shall know" (John 7:17*a*). "The illumination of obedience" (Brooks)! Except in a mission church just getting under way, almost every congregation has in its membership all the potential leaders and workers necessary to carry forward any project in accord with the will of God. Ideally, all that the minister has to do is guide laymen in setting up goals, and in choosing the best available persons to lead in the work. Then he can bid these friends Godspeed as lay leaders, and resolve to keep his hands off everything the Lord has commissioned someone else to do for His glory.

Lack of a Working Plan

Elsewhere I have written at length about the advantages of such a plan, with special reference to work for the pulpit. Here I shall deal rather with certain disadvantages in not planning. In general they accord with the findings of the foremost medical writer in modern times. Sir William Osler used to declare that in his profession there were two sorts of conscientious, hardworking men: the one who planned his work and then followed his plan, with an increasing sense of satisfaction, over against the one whose everyday labors led him hither and thither, with a growing sense of futility and frustration.

In every part of an active ministry the absence of a working program leads to loss of time, energy, and patience. The lack of a high controlling purpose tends to create and foster a feeling of dissatisfaction, with resulting moods far remote from the peace of heart that a minister needs in making ready to pray in public, to preach, or to counsel with a friend in distress of soul. The same holds true in his work as a practical leader of others. The mission of a pastor, as we have seen, consists largely in letting the truth, the goodness, and the radiance of God shine out on others through the minister's Christlike personality. If so, any planlessness that partially makes him unfit for his highest usefulness calls for contrition and reform.

For example, take a hard-working pastor in a community near Princeton. In the seminary library, week after week, he would read assiduously, and take careful notes. Always he singled out worthy volumes on the subjects and passages of the two sermons for next Sunday. Not having a self-made program for reading and preaching, he seldom had time to deal adequately with any subject and passage about which he preached. After several years of such diligent drudgery he told me that he had made a sad discovery. He had not mastered any one of those standard books, and he did not have an adequate knowledge of any important subject or passage about which he had preached. His hop-skip-and-jump way of reading and preaching had brought him little joy, and no sense of growth. He had been living from hand to mouth, and often he had preached without feeling prepared.

Much the same principle applies to everything else that a minister ought to do. In calling on the sick, in counseling with a distraught soul, in visiting a home that needs pastoral care, in dealing with a committee, and in a host of related activities, he can follow a system of his own devising, and thus form habits of orderly procedure. Or else he toils by fits and starts, or by fuss and stops, which tend to make his ministry a thing of "shreds and patches," rather than an artistic whole. Sometimes a man of this hit-and-miss kind wonders why people do not notify him about cases of serious illness or other calamity. They in turn wonder why they should call for the presence of a man who never has mastered "the art of visiting the sick." As with every other art, this one calls for a working knowledge of certain principles, which a planless pastor never takes time to learn.

The increasing seriousness of this matter appears in a current series of Lyman Beecher Lectures at Yale. The speaker, Joseph Sittler, worthily represents the Lutheran clergy, who have won distinction as pastors. From their home ministers and in the seminary many Lutheran ministers have learned to systematize their work, and then to do it with zest. On the contrary, one of those Lectures dealt with "The Maceration of the Minister." To macerate means to "chop into small pieces." "That this is what is happening to thousands of ministers does not have to be argued or established. It needs only to be violently stated. The minister's time, his focused sense of vocation, his vision of his central task, his mental life, and his contemplative acreage—these are under the chopper."

Professor Sittler speaks from personal experience and from wide observation. After thirteen years in the pastorate he became a seminary professor. Now his former students tell him that as pastors they suffer from a sense of "vocational guilt," "so strong, so clear, so deeply sunk . . . that no diminution of hours or other rearrangement of outer life can have a decisive effect. This sense of guilt has observable content. A minister has been ordained to an Office; too often he ends by running an office. He was solemnly ordained to the ministry in Christ's Church. Most of the men whom I know really want to be what they intended and prepared for. They have ended up in a sort of dizzy occupational oscillation." [6]

[6] *Christian Century*, June 10, 1959.

A Way Out of the Maze

In full view of all these facts and fears, what do I propose, constructively? Nothing revolutionary, or even startling. Rather do I advocate a prayerful return to the ideals of Holy Scripture, as they have often been tested throughout church history, and are now being followed by more than a few busy pastors. Among my own wide circle of friends and acquaintances in churches large, small, and of medium size, no small number of men have so planned life and work as to put the first thing first, and that with increasing satisfaction. Each of them has planned his work in a way largely his own, and much different from mine. All are alike in making a determined stand for a spiritual ministry, and in holding fast to this ideal, whatever the cost. Without boasting, any one of them could make this practical statement about his life purpose:

"By the grace of God I aim to be a good man, a good pastor, a good counselor, a good leader in worship, a good preacher, and a good steward of all my opportunity as the responsible head of the teaching and the work of this congregation." This type of apostolic ministry (Acts 6:4) is what every high-minded pastor wishes to enjoy, and what the majority of his lay officers and leaders desire from their minister. "It is simply not true," according to Sittler, "that the parish demands of its minister that he become simply an executive officer of multiple activities." Amen! If the large majority of the people love and trust their pastor, as they yearn to do, they tend to accept as right and proper whatever he does in the use of his time. But they do not enjoy or admire what Sittler terms "catch-as-catch-can preaching," or neglect of their souls by an expert operator of ecclesiastical machinery.

Among the various forms of ministerial usefulness, which one ought to receive the priority? The one in which the pastor ought to be engaged at the time! A minister with "the mind of Christ" ought to feel equally at home and happy while caring for his own inner being, shepherding any of the flock, guiding the congregation in prayer, preaching the kerygma, administering the sacraments, or ordinances, or leading in the local work of the Kingdom. If the Lord wishes him to lead in raising money for church improvements, or in any other "spiritual work," he thanks God for the privilege. Once a father with four sons asked their mother which of them she had loved most when they were little. At once she replied, "The one I held in my arms!" And so in love for a man's work as a pastor,

> It is the heart and not the brain
> That to the highest doth attain.

As a professor of homiletics I may at times have seemed not to appreciate a minister's other work as a "pastoral director." If so, I feel sorry. According to Holy Writ a shepherd ought to lead the flock. This means that he ought to hold himself responsible for all its manifold activities. Unfortunately, the facts about ministers in small churches do not often appear in my source books. But when I read about young George W. Truett I find that in a small church at Dallas he led people according to simple plans of his own making. Later in life, with eight thousand members, a staff of expert associates, and a host of loyal volunteer workers, he still kept his eyes mainly on the things that mattered most for time and eternity. So did Spurgeon and Brooks and many another who excelled as the responsible head of a local church.

Doctrinally, the whole matter goes back to belief in the Providence or Sovereignty of God. More than a hundred years ago (1858) Horace Bushnell preached a sermon, "Every Man's Life a Plan of God." [7] Because of its continued influence this message has become known as probably the most noteworthy utterance of the American pulpit so far. Here follows the central proposition, or motif, with a change in two words, now in brackets. What Bushnell said to the lay hearer I apply to a

[7] See *Sermons for the New Life*, various editions, sermon one.

pastor: "God has a definite life-plan for every [Christian minister], girding him, visibly or invisibly, for some exact thing, which it will be the significance and glory of his life to have accomplished."

A little later in the sermon the Hartford divine declared:

> Every [Christian minister] has a complete and perfect plan cherished for him in the heart of God, a divine biography marked out. . . . This life, rightly unfolded, will be a complete and beautiful whole, an experience led on by God; . . . a drama cast in the mold of a perfect art, with no part missing; a divine study that shall forever unfold in wondrous beauty the love and faithfulness of God. What a thought for every [Christian minister] to cherish! What dignity does it lend to life! What support does it bring to the trials of life! . . . There ought never to be a discouraged or uncheerful man in the [Christian ministry].

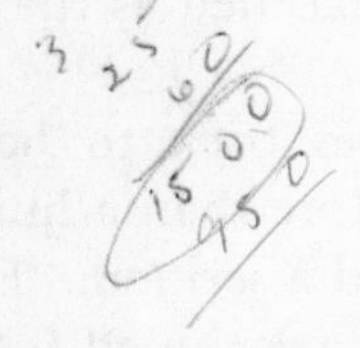

CHAPTER XVII

Insufficient Trust

IN THE OPENING CHAPTER OF THIS BOOK WE CONSIDERED THE IDEALS of a minister who keeps growing. In the next eight chapters we considered his opportunities to grow while doing his regular work. Then we looked at various obstacles that tend to check or stop his growth. Now at last we face a resulting question, fraught with difficulty: "Why do these obstacles seriously interfere with the growth of a good man's soul?" Near the end of my book on *Pastoral Leadership* I discussed these matters with reference to Christian love as the all-inclusive secret of ministerial growth. Love here refers to Christ's love for us, supremely on the Cross. (II Cor. 5:14, R.S.V.) Whenever His love "controls" heart and life, a minister can keep growing in likeness to his Lord, and in favor with God's people. How simple, and how sublime!

Much the same practical philosophy relates to trust in God. This term here means reliance on Him for wisdom, for strength, and for guidance in doing His holy will for the local church and the wider concerns of His Kingdom. If anyone asks why the stress in this chapter falls on trust, rather than faith, the answer is that we are later to think about a pastor's trust in his people, and in himself. Some of us employ the term faith only with reference to a feeling of dependence on the Father, the Son, and the Holy Spirit. But let us not bicker about words! Whatever the term, let us take for granted that every minister ought to keep growing more Christlike through the increase of his trust in the Heavenly Father.

By way of testing this hypothesis any reader can make a list of his favorite ministerial and missionary heroes. Starting with the Hebrew Hall of Fame (Heb. 11) and coming down to our own day, which men have impressed him most by their spiritual growth from youth over into old age, and by their lasting influence over the Church at large? He will find that these men have differed from each other as much as stars in the sky, but that all of these heroes have been alike in trusting God as their only Source of truth, grace, and power. In short, a pastor's growth in Christlikeness depends on the quality and the degree of his trust in the Heavenly Father. This working philosophy has undergirded the present book.

Lack of Trust in God's Providence

On the contrary, think about a procession of men equally able and promising who have not kept growing in Christlikeness. Any lover of biography can make a fairly long list of persons like King Saul and Judas Iscariot. Saul, for example, started his career with the most brilliant promise. Then gradually his powers declined until at last he met a tragic death, "unwept, unhonored, and unsung." As for Judas, few have sunk so low. From his time until today more than a few men called of God to the noblest mission on earth have fallen away from truth and honor. For a well-known example turn to Peter Abelard (d. 1142), one of the most brilliant figures in the history of the Church. His letters to Heloise and her replies to him "belong to world literature." To at least one reader his part of the correspondence displays callous cruelty and colossal conceit. If so, he reminds us again that pride often leads to other deadly sins.

Opinions differ about the number of such men now in the ministry. I for one believe that the number and proportion of such persons has been lower among ministerial recruits since World War II than at any time in our century. But even if there were only one such case, that one would serve as a danger signal. From some such point of view Clarence E. Macartney once spoke about unworthy ministers of an earlier generation. In Miller Chapel at Princeton Seminary he delivered a searching message about "Your Unknown Self" (II Kings 8:13). After he had finished all that he would have said to laymen, the Pittsburgh divine added another paragraph. In it he warned seminary men about the perils and the pitfalls of the life work in which they would soon engage. These perils and pitfalls, let us note, still yawn before every minister who fails to trust in God. Now listen to Macartney, a lifelong student of church history and ministerial biography:

> Ten years after graduation the annals of any seminary class would make awesome and heart-breaking reading. Some had hardly put on their armor before they fell into perversions of Christianity. Others were overtaken and overwhelmed by temptation, and fell into sin—a reproach to Christ, a burden and a curse to themselves, all their lights put out in darkness, and the glorious shield of their consecration vilely cast away, as though they had not been anointed with holy oil. . . .
>
> My soul, be on thy guard,
> Ten thousand foes arise! [1]

Every one of those men fell through lack of trust in God's Providence and Grace. Here let us think about Providence in terms of the Westminster *Shorter Catechism:* "God's works of Providence are His most holy, wise, and powerful, preserving and governing all His creatures and all their actions." If anyone prefers to think of God's Sovereignty, that idea will fit equally well. The degree to which a minister lets either or both truths guide and restrain all his life and activity will go far to determine the extent and the direction of his growth in grace, or of his decline in Christlikeness.

On the basis of trust in God every minister ought to work out his own practical philosophy of life and service. Of course he should know that he can "work out" only what the Lord by grace has first worked into his heart and life (Phil. 2:12-13).

[1] From a private manuscript, by permission of the author.

He ought also to remember that the Holy Spirit as the Paraclete ever stands by to strengthen and enforce the trust that may falter and threaten to fail. If there were need for doing so now, we could pass in review the various obstacles that have loomed up in preceding chapters, and show that every one of them gives way before the minister who does not in his own strength confide, but trusts in the power and the wisdom of Almighty God. "Not by might nor by power, but by my Spirit, says the Lord of hosts. What are you, O great mountain? Before Zerubbabel [God's leader of men] you shall become a plain." (Zech. 4:6*b*-7*a* R.S.V.)

These ideas about personal growth through trusting in the Providence of God ought to bring special assurance and hope to a young minister. Fortunately, he need not wait until he is elderly before he begins to seem Christlike. For a message of cheer he may turn again to that sermon from Horace Bushnell about being girded of God for a life of increasing usefulness and Christlikeness. The preacher is addressing a young man, who may be an inexperienced pastor:

> This is the day of hope to you. All your best opportunities are still before you. Now you are laying your plans for the future. Why not lay them in God? Who has planned so wisely and faithfully as He? Believe that you are girded by your God for a holy and great calling. [Come] to Him, consecrate your life to Him, knowing assuredly that He will lead you into just that life which is your highest honor and blessing.

Lack of Trust in God's People

A minister's failure to keep growing may also be due to his lack of trust in God's people. When the Lord calls a minister to serve in a local church He surrounds His servant with a throng of potential helpers in growth toward Christlikeness. As we have already seen more than once, if the incoming leader accepts them in the right spirit, and continues to deal with them as God's messengers of grace, he will find a growing number of helpers in every good work, and sharers in every Christlike joy. From such a happy point of view many a former pastor can write to friends far away: "I thank God upon every remembrance of you" (Phil. 1:3). On the other hand, if he fails to trust them, and enlist them for Kingdom service, he may never dream how much they could have helped him spiritually if he had opened his heart and let the light of God shine into his life through the loving kindness of God's lay messengers.

Ideally, an incoming pastor looks on the "new" people with glad expectations. He wishes to know them well that he may love them much. He believes in them and expects from them much in the way of enthusiastic service. Such a spirit of "apostolic optimism" quickly becomes contagious, and it continues to spread among the people as long as their minister keeps trusting these fellow laborers for Christ. In other words, a pastoral leader worthy of the name excels in human relations. He inspires loyalty, which is another name for trust. In the terms of Josiah Royce, a foremost philosopher of yesterday, loyalty means "the willing, practical, thorough-going devotion of a person to a cause as that cause is embodied in a person."

The cause to which pastor and people gladly give supreme devotion is the Kingdom (Matt. 6:33). The Person who calls forth and increases their loyalty is King Jesus. But practically, being human and frail, many of God's children think of the Kingdom in terms of the home church, and what it represents in community and world betterment. They also think of loyalty to Christ in terms of devotion to the minister and his wife. However much he may fail to get their affections orientated aright, he should continue to love and trust these little ones in God's household. By dealing with them tenderly and kindly he can gradually lead short-sighted friends to put Christ and His Kingdom first.

Alas, not every pastor, able and conscientious, excels in human relations. Not every would-be shepherd understands sheep, or knows how to care for lambs. Our Risen Lord told impetuous young Peter that the best way to prove his love and loyalty for his Master was to feed the sheep. Among the pastors whom I have known as having a "hard time with their people," the difficulties and the friction have usually arisen, not so much by what he said in the pulpit, but by what he did in dealing with officers and members. The fault may lie on both sides, or mainly with the people. Even so, many a discontented pastor has failed to fulfill the promise of his youth. This failure has been due mainly to lack of skill and care in cultivating God's people as a means of grace to their pastor.

Fortunately, such a man can learn his lesson and change his ways before it is too late. For a Bible example of a strong leader who begins to grow in grace through learning to rely on lay helpers, turn again to Moses. In a forbidding field he seems to be "losing out" as a master of human relations. From an elderly "in-law" the leader of that large "congregation" learns to let other men do all that their God-given powers enable them to do for His glory. Then he has time and energy to do well what the Lord has reserved for him as the responsible leader. Long ere now this may have begun to sound like an "old, old story." But remember that through the opening of his eyes and the change in his methods Moses gained a new hold on the hearts of a disaffected people. Because of these new relations he became far more saintly. Indeed, when he died the Lord had to keep secret the place of his burial. Otherwise the people who had once resented his leadership would have been tempted to make his burial place a shrine for the worship of God, or of Moses.

The apostles in Jerusalem afford other examples of comparatively young men who found in human relations a means of growing Christlike. Even under the leadership of the foremost apostles the local church began to suffer through bickerings among women. They belonged to diverse peoples, racially, and they quarreled about money. In more than one church such a threatened rift has led to a pastor's stomach ulcers, and stomach ulcers do not cause a growth in piety. But the apostles decided to trust the people. Calling them together, the ministerial leaders explained the local situation, pointed out the need for a change in working methods, and led the congregation to elect seven men, who seem to have been deacons (Acts 6:1-8).

With their Greek names the seven appear to have represented the group to whom the aggrieved widows belonged. In Hawaii, the fiftieth state of our Union, two of the men first elected to high office represented the native people. Would that in every election of state or church the leaders trusted the people so fully, and likewise kept them informed. In Jerusalem the new lay officers were deeply spiritual. Hence they did their work so well that the tension seems to have disappeared. Then the "ministers" could devote themselves anew to the work for which the Lord Jesus had trained them before "the Day of the Cross." Is it any wonder that the apostles kept on growing more like Him?

Those newly-elected deacons looked on the serving of tables —an orderly arrangement for the relief of the worthy poor—as a God-given way of doing spiritual work. The deacons must have recalled a vision of Zechariah (14:20*b*) about an ideal church of the morrow: "The pots in the house of the Lord shall be as holy as the bowls before the altar." While busy as one of God's almoners in the local church Stephen did the will of the Lord as truly as later when he delivered a mighty sermon and then became the first Christian martyr. Another of those almoners, Deacon Philip, did the will of God as truly as when he afterward led in a revival at the city of Samaria and then won for Christ the Ethiopian "Secretary of the Treasury."

As often in recent times, those two men developed God-given powers through using them wisely in the service of men. Because they kept growing they could later reach out and engage in a larger ministry. Here we have an example of what our Lord teaches in the parable about the talents (Matt. 25: 14-30). This parable shows how the Lord trusts the men who work for Him, and rewards each of them by allowing him to do more work. If once in a while He finds among the working force a do-less drone, this Bible fact ought to encourage a minister who fails to enlist a potential worker. All the while the leader sent from God operates on the principle of relying on potential workers far from ideal. Thus he gradually learns the answer to the question before us in this book: "How can a minister keep growing like his Lord?"

Paul sets forth this truth in terms of the church as a body (I Cor. 12 *et al.*) In Corinth he did not have perfect material with which to work. Still he trusted those people, and he won out with the majority. Like other Bible figures of speech, this one holds good only with reference to what it was intended to teach. To the pastor it means that in order to keep the church body well and strong he ought to see that every member has work to do according to his God-given powers. Weak and faulty as lay folk often seem, their leader ought to trust them, one by one. How else did our Lord deal with young Simon Peter, when he was weak as water and shifting as sand? "Thou shalt be a man of rock, a strong servant of God and a worthy leader of men." Through open expression of belief in young Simon our Lord began to make him strong. Through belief in many a weakling today a pastor can become more like his Lord.

Lack of Trust in God's Pastor

This next idea is difficult to state aright. It has to do with Christian self-respect, self-assurance, and self-direction, always under the guidance and restraint of the Holy Spirit. Today as of old more than one potential leader with an "inferiority complex" needs to hear the Lord speaking to him: "Stand upon thy feet and I will speak to thee" (Ezek. 2:1). In other words, God calls such a man to assume the spiritual leadership of several hundred persons, "scattered as sheep without a shepherd." The Lord expects His undershepherd to speak and act with an authority not his own. As long as a minister puts first the glory of his Lord, and second the welfare of the people, he need never fear lest he carry self-confidence too far. Only by exercise of God-given powers can he grow like the One who set His face like a flint (Isa. 50:7*c*), going up to Jerusalem, there to die.

At times a heaven-sent leader may seem to have a dual personality, though never one "split." In dealing with the weak, the helpless, and the guilty, he may resemble Hosea, Jeremiah, or Paul, no one of whom felt ashamed to weep over the unworthy. Through the glint of unshed tears such a leader can win and hold the esteem and the love of saints and sinners. But when an occasion calls for a prophetic voice speaking against tyranny, oppression, and cruelty, this man displays rugged strength, iron courage, and deathless perseverance. Why so? Because he trusts in himself as an authorized representative of the Almighty, and as the appointed leader of God's people.

In the history of the Church such God-given self-assurance has marked the career of almost every leader at whom we have looked. For a study in the life of a leader who had a tender heart, and yet never flinched when the hour called for a note of authority, turn to the popular biography by Ronald H. Bainton, *Here I Stand, A Life of Martin Luther* (1950). In like manner every pastor needs to show the gentler qualities of our holy faith, and still at times display the boldness of a lion. Whatever the call of duty in an hour of need, a Christlike man never fails to rely on his God-given powers. With the apostle Paul, and without boasting, a self-assured leader often says with thanksgiving to God: "I can do all things in him who strengthens me" (Phil. 4:13). Herein lies one of the Lord's appointed ways to grow Christlike.

If it were necessary we could look back over various ministerial obstacles and see how every one of them tends to give way before the man who has the right sort of trust in God, in others, and in himself as God's servant and their leader. We could set forth an array of spiritual heroes and note that every one of them had the sort of assurance that in a less spiritual person would seem like presumption. As an example, turn again to the apostle Peter. While in the "seminary" he often displayed the wrong sort of self-reliance, which led him to blurt out words far from discreet, and to boast about superiority over the other disciples. Indeed, he even dared to rebuke his Lord!

At the end of his "seminary" days Peter must have seemed like a pitiful "candidate" for leadership in the Apostolic Church. But after he had seen the Redeemer die, and had received the Holy Spirit, Peter became a new man "in Christ." First as an apostle with power, and later as a saint with piety (I Peter), this man stood out as a living example of how to combine Christian humility with holy boldness. Instead of his former "excess baggage"—pride, arrogance, and lack of love for others—he showed us how to keep growing in grace by trusting in God, in others, and in himself. Toward the end of a life during which he continued to grow more like his Lord, Peter wrote a sentence that could have served as his own motto: "Grow in the grace and knowledge of our Lord and Saviour" (II Pet. 3:18).

In a form still more lofty this "Apostle of Christian Hope" appeals to men chosen of God for leadership in local churches: "I exhort the elders among you, as a fellow elder and a witness of the sufferings of Christ, as well as a partaker of the glory that is to be revealed. Tend the flock of God that is your charge, not by constraint but willingly, not for shameful gain but eagerly, not as domineering over those in your charge but being examples to the flock. And when the chief Shepherd is manifested you will obtain the unfading crown of glory.

"Likewise you that are younger be subject to the elders. Clothe yourselves, all of you, with humility toward one another.

. . . Cast all your anxieties on him, for he cares for you. . . . And the God of all grace, who has called you to his eternal glory in Christ, will himself restore, establish, and strengthen you. To Him be the dominion for ever and ever. Amen." (I Pet. 5: 5-11 A.S.V.)

Related Readings

The Ministry

Calkins, Raymond. *The Romance of the Ministry*. Boston: Pilgrim Press, 1944. Like most of the men listed below, an able evangelical liberal.

Edwards, Jonathan. *A Treatise Concerning Religious Affections. Works*, Vol. II, ed. by John E. Smith. New Haven: Yale University Press, 1959. The ablest of all the books listed.

Hiltner, Seward. *Preface to Pastoral Theology*. Nashville: Abingdon Press, 1958. Scholarly. Philosophical, not practical.

Jenkins, Daniel. *The Protestant Ministry*. An English theologian who knows and loves the States.

Johnson, Paul E. *Psychology of Religion*, rev. and enlarged. Nashville: Abingdon Press, 1959. Able. Interesting. Helpful.

Kemp, Charles F. *Preparing for the Ministry*. St. Louis: Bethany Press, 1959.

Marty, Martin E. *The New Shape of American Religion*. New York: Harper & Bros., 1959. Often brilliant. Searching. Provocative.

Niebuhr, H. Richard. *The Purpose of the Church and Its Ministry*. New York: Harper & Bros., 1956. First part of a report based on exhaustive studies of theological education in North America.

——— and Daniel D. Williams, eds., *The Ministry in Historical Perspective*, Vol. II. New York: Harper & Bros., 1956.

———, D. D. Williams, and James M. Gustafson, *The Advancement of Theological Education*, Vol. III. New York: Harper & Bros., 1957. The three call for careful reading.

Rodenmayer, Robert N. *We Have This Ministry*. New York: Harper & Bros., 1959.

Thornton, Martin. *Pastoral Theology: A Reorientation*. New York: The Macmillan Co., 1957. A British Anglican. Able. Not practical.

The Minister

Allport, Gordon W. *Becoming: Basic Considerations for a Psychology of Personality*. New Haven: Yale University Press, 1955. Secular. Able.

RELATED READINGS

Baxter, Richard. *The Reformed Pastor,* 1656, ed. John T. Wilkinson. Chicago: A. R. Allenson, 1950. A Protestant classic.

Blackwood, Carolyn P. *The Pastor's Wife.* Philadelphia: Westminster Press, 1951.

Harmon, Nolan B., Jr. *Ministerial Ethics and Etiquette.* Nashville, Abingdon Press, 1950. Apex edition, 1959. Practical wisdom from a Methodist bishop, formerly an editor.

Hedley, George P. *The Minister Behind the Scenes.* New York: The Macmillan Co., 1956. Informal.

Herbert, George. *A Priest in the Temple,* or *The Country Parson,* 1652. Many editions. Delightfully human and helpful.

Hiltner, Seward. *The Christian Shepherd.* Nashville: Abingdon Press, 1959.

Johnson, Paul E. *Personality and Religion.* Nashville: Abingdon Press, 1957. Good ideas. The King's English.

Jones, E. Stanley. *Christian Maturity.* Nashville: Abingdon Press, 1957. Chiefly for laymen. A living example of his thesis.

Neill, Stephen C. *Fulfill Thy Ministry.* New York: Harper & Bros., 1952. A gifted Anglican bishop, formerly a missionary to India.

Oates, Wayne E. *Religious Dimensions of Personality.* New York: Association Press, 1957. Scholarly. Solid. Not popular.

Rendtorff, Heinrich. *The Pastor's Personal Life.* Minneapolis: Augsburg Publishing House, 1959. Lutherans often excel as pastors.

Schuette, Walter E. *The Minister's Personal Guide.* New York: Harper & Bros., 1953. Practical. General. Many good ideas.

Tournier, Paul. *The Meaning of Persons* (tr.) New York: Harper & Bros. Secular. Highly praised.

Turnbull, Ralph G. *A Minister's Obstacles.* Westwood, N. J.: Fleming H. Revell Co., paper ed., 1959. Conservative. Practical.

West, Robert Frederick. *Light Beyond Shadows.* New York: The Macmillan Co., 1959. A minister's breakdown and recovery.

Spiritual Life

Baillie, John. *A Diary of Private Prayer.* New York: Charles Scribner's Sons, 1948. Best known current book in the field.

Barclay, William. *A Book of Everyday Prayers.* New York: Harper & Bros., 1960. Chiefly for laymen, by an able Scottish scholar.

Bauman, Edward W. *Intercessory Prayer.* Philadelphia: Westminster Press, 1958. Good for both ministers and laymen.

Brightman, Edgar S. *The Spiritual Life.* Nashville: Abingdon Press, 1942. An able Boston University professor of philosophy.

Doberstein, John W. *Minister's Prayer Book.* Philadelphia: Muhlenberg Press, 1959.

Law, William. *A Serious Call to a Devout and Holy Life,* 1729, abridged and ed. by John W. Meister *et al.* Philadelphia: Westminster Press, 1955. A Protestant classic. Appears once again, for emphasis.

Luther, Martin. *The Letters of Spiritual Counsel* (trans.), ed. by Theodore G. Tappert. Philadelphia: Westminster Press, 1955. Unlike others in these lists, Luther had a big heart.

Thomas, G. Ernest. *Spiritual Life in the New Testament.* Westwood, N. J.: Fleming H. Revell Co., 1955. Simple. Pleasing. Helpful.

Weatherhead, Leslie D. *A Private House of Prayer.* Nashville: Abingdon Press, 1959.

White, Reginald E. O. *Prayer Is the Secret.* New York: Harper & Bros., 1959. Not for ministers, but has some suggestions.

The Minister's Work

Allan, Tom. *The Face of My Parish.* New York: Harper & Bros., 1957. Community evangelism by the local church. Inspirational.

Burns, James. *Revivals, Their Laws and Leaders,* 1909. Grand Rapids: Baker Book House, reprint, 1960. Able biographical studies.

Cabot, R. C. and Dicks, R. L. *The Art of Ministering to the Sick.* A classic. Study Chap. II.

Church Management. A monthly magazine for ministers, Cleveland, Ohio.

Davies, Horton. *Christian Worship, Its History and Meaning.* Nashville: Abingdon Press, 1957.

Doniger, Simon, ed. *The Minister's Consultation Clinic.* Great Neck, N. Y.: Channel Press, 1957.

Gregory the Great. *The Pastoral Rule* (tr.) A classic. Various editions.

Hulme, William E. *Counseling and Theology.* Philadelphia: Muhlenberg Press, 1956. Able. Helpful.

Johnson, Paul E. *Psychology of Pastoral Care.* Nashville: Abingdon Press, 1953. Excellent of its kind.

Jones, Edgar D. *The Royalty of the Pulpit, Lyman Beecher Lectures on Preaching.* New York: Harper & Bros., 1951.

McCabe, Joseph E., *The Power of God in a Parish Program.* Philadelphia: Westminster Press, 1959. Wise methods, not stereotyped. Most suggestive.

May, Rollo. *The Art of Counseling.* Nashville: Abingdon Press; Apex edition, 1957. Sane and wholesome.

Miller, Paul M. *Group Dynamics in Evangelism.* Scottdale, Pennsylvania: Herald Press, 1958. A Mennonite author.

RELATED READINGS

Pastoral Psychology. Great Neck, New York. Monthly magazine for ministers.

Pulpit Digest. Great Neck, New York. Monthly magazine for ministers.

Sangster, W. E. *Power in Preaching*. Nashville: Abingdon Press, 1958. A foremost London Wesleyan preacher and writer. Perhaps his ablest book.

Underhill, Evelyn. *Worship*. New York: Harper & Bros.; Torch book edition, 1957. Gifted Anglican writer on mysticism and other subjects.

Vieth, Paul H. *The Church School: The Organization, Administration, and supervision of Christian Education in the Local Church*. Philadelphia: Christian Education Press, 1957. Probably best work of its kind. What a pastor needs to know.

Index of Persons and Subjects

INDEX OF PERSONS AND SUBJECTS

INDEX OF PERSONS AND SUBJECTS